P9-DMV-697

I CAN READ YOU LIKE A BOOK

how to spot the
messages and emotions
people are *really* sending
with their body language

Gregory Hartley and Maryann Karinch
authors of *How to Spot a Liar*

CAREER
PRESS
Franklin Lakes, NJ

I CAN READ YOU LIKE A BOOK
EDITED AND TYPESET BY GINA TALUCCI
Printed in the U.S.A. by Book-mart Press

To order this title, please call toll-free 1-800-CAREER-1 (NJ and Canada: 201-848-0310) to order using VISA or MasterCard, or for further information on books from Career Press.

The Career Press, Inc., 3 Tice Road, PO Box 687,
Franklin Lakes, NJ 07417
www.careerpress.com

Library of Congress Cataloging-in-Publication Data

Hartley, Gregory.
   I can read you like a book : how to spot the messages and emotions people are really sending with their body language / by Gregory Hartley and Maryann Karinch.
      p. cm.
   Includes Index.
   ISBN-13: 978-156414-941-1
   ISBN-10: 1-56414-941-2
     1. Body language. 2. Interpersonal communication. 3. Nonverbal communication. I. Karinch, Maryann. II. Title.
BF637.N66H38 2007
153.6′9--dc22

                                            2006038158

To my mom and dad, and Betty and Marlin Hartley, for sacrificing so that I could do and become things they could never imagine.

—Greg

To Jim, Mom, and Karl, for your unwavering support and energetic love.

—Maryann

DEDICATION

Thank you to Jim McCormick for giving me loving support, despite my ridiculous schedule, and for providing keen
insights along the way. As always, I want to thank my mother
and brother, Karl, for being ready with encouraging words.
I am also grateful for the enthusiasm and support we have
received from the Career Press team, specifically, Ron Fry,
Michael Pye, Kristen Parkes, Laurie Kelly-Pye, Gina Talucci
and Linda Rienecker. Also, my dear friends whose good
thinking and professions enable them to offer me practical
guidance, especially Patti Mengers and David Kozinski.
Thank you, too, Scott and Eliza Ferzeley, for allowing us to
use a picture of your smiling son, Caden, in the book. And
to our talented model, Kurtis Kelly. I also want to acknowledge the experts whose research and writings helped
provide deeper understanding of some of the key issues

A
C
K
N
O
W
L
E
D
G
M
E
N
T
S

covered in the book, particularly Candace Gordon and Dr. Louann Brizendine. And thank you, Greg, for being such a fun and enlightening partner!

—Maryann Karinch

First and foremost, thanks to the volunteers who defend our country in time of war for too little pay and uncertain futures. May we tread carefully when criticizing national policy lest we injure one of these heroes.

This book would not exist if not for Michael Dobson, who encouraged me to share my thoughts with you and introduced me to Maryann. This book could not happen without all the support Dina gives me. Jeffrey has changed the way I see the world and myself and for that I am grateful. Rick Croley expands my mind by challenging me to think in new ways about old topics through wonderful conversation. Thank you to Jim McCormick for insight, camaraderie, and support. Maryann, this book has been a pleasure to create thanks to you.

—Greg Hartley

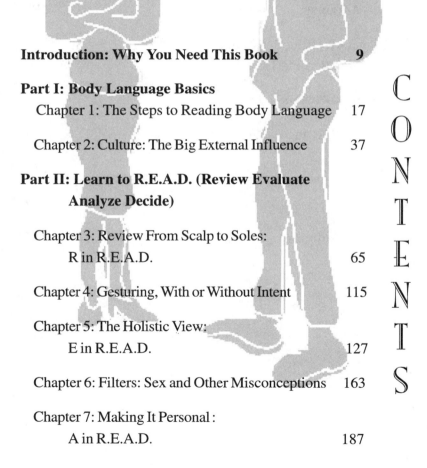

Introduction: Why You Need This Book   9

Part I: Body Language Basics
    Chapter 1: The Steps to Reading Body Language   17

    Chapter 2: Culture: The Big External Influence   37

Part II: Learn to R.E.A.D. (Review Evaluate Analyze Decide)

    Chapter 3: Review From Scalp to Soles:
        R in R.E.A.D.   65

    Chapter 4: Gesturing, With or Without Intent   115

    Chapter 5: The Holistic View:
        E in R.E.A.D.   127

    Chapter 6: Filters: Sex and Other Misconceptions   163

    Chapter 7: Making It Personal:
        A in R.E.A.D.   187

C
O
N
T
E
N
T
S

Part III: Applying the Skill

Chapter 8: Politicians, Pundits, and Stars:
    D in R.E.A.D.   209

Chapter 9: The Man in the Street   231

Chapter 10: Using Body Language to Your
    Advantage in Business   247

Chapter 11: Using Body Language in
    Your Personal Life   261

Part IV: Conclusion

Chapter 12: Using R.E.A.D.   273

Glossary   **277**

Index   **279**

About the Authors   **285**

Why You Need This Book

Do you want to:

⇒ Know the early warning signs of rage?

⇒ Elect people who really know what they're talking about?

⇒ Establish rapport quickly with customers?

⇒ Contribute juicy insights to discussions about your favorite celebrities?

⇒ Recognize love at first sight?

⇒ Become the salesperson everyone wants to talk to?

⇒ Be the actor who nails every scene, and always gets the call back?

This book will satisfy desires similar to those listed while I give you a step-by-step guide to reading body language and using it to affect emotions, including your own and other people's.

Have you ever walked into a room and had someone greet you in a personal way, but you didn't recognize her? Instantly, no matter how well your voice mimics familiarity, that individual knows you have no idea who she is. Not a great way to start a meeting, wedding reception, or a class reunion. If you knew little about body language, you could easily convince her that you did recognize her.

If you knew a little more, you could put her at ease so quickly that she would tell you about herself, giving you distinct advantages in whatever conversation or negotiations ensued.

Turn the tables: She does not know who you are, but uses the fact that most people cannot admit memory lapse to get closer to you.

Most people who are good at reading body language can't tell you how they do it. They have not codified their instinctive ability, so the skills are not transferable. My edge over other interrogators, and the reason I was eventually hired to train them, has always been understanding why certain techniques work and, being able to replicate the effect. It's a sense of causality between action and reaction.

You will not find my approach to the subject of body language, or even much of the vocabulary I use, in psychology textbooks. My academic background is not what shaped my expertise. It's my experience in the field of battle, in conducting countless training exercises at the SERE (Survival Evasion Resistance Escape) school, in business negotiations, in conducting interviews of executive candidates for corporations. In other words, real life; not the lab. Nevertheless, my approach in the way I go about integrating new knowledge and refining my techniques is scientific. If you have this kind of methodical approach to reading body language, you can also develop the ability to use it in reverse. You can control your shadowy memory of body language to influence another person's behavior. As an interrogator, I get what I want by manipulating body language and emotions together, both mine and the other person's. This is the crux of what interrogators do.

With the kind of skills I have in reading and using body language, though, I sometimes daydream about other work I might do. Right now, it's summer, and I was thinking I might have a second career as a spy for a baseball team because pitchers' movements often bleed so much information. Pulling ears may be a deliberate signal to the catcher, but other body language rituals can tell you about the degree of confidence or stress, uncertainty about whether or not the type of pitch is the right pitch, and even residual embarrassment from the last bad pitch.

Or maybe I'll grow up to be a negotiator in big business, for management or labor. Humans project what we are thinking, telegraphing the next move, and that allows me to manipulate the train of thought.

Or maybe I'll get a more glamorous job, such as becoming the body language coach for the latest crime show.

When you get the skills, what are you going to do with them?

— Greg Hartley

Flow of the Book

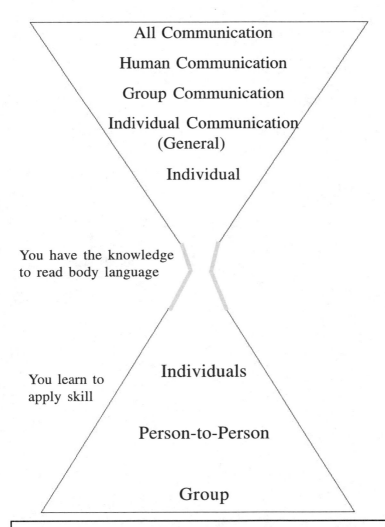

All Communication

Human Communication

Group Communication

Individual Communication
(General)

Individual

You have the knowledge
to read body language

You learn to
apply skill

Individuals

Person-to-Person

Group

You learn to apply the skill to yourself: Extreme self-control

Body Language
Basics

P
A
R
T

I

The Steps to Reading Body Language

Primitive man had a repertoire of survival skills that included reading body language. Etiquette and culture have blunted that natural human ability. Add to those factors the complexity of spoken language and modern conventions related to body language—stock gestures we see all the time in movies and TV—and the result is this: few people today can read body language well.

Most of the time, we don't even know what our own bodies are doing. Human body language is more closely tied to ritual than planned behavior. I don't think about how to pick up my glass when I drink, how to hold my fork, or start my car. Our brains are so complex, with multiple subprograms running at all times, that it is difficult to have complete control over every twitch and tap. It is difficult for us to even remember what we've done if the action has reached the point of ritual or habit.

I teach professionals in finance and sales to read body language, as well as investigators, interrogators, special operations forces, and security professionals. For all of the latter groups, the survival of their careers, if not their lives, may depend on that ability.

In the following chapters, I will introduce you to a system I call R.E.A.D.—Review, Evaluate, Analyze, Decide—an in-depth version of the course I teach government and military students in my body language classes. This is the same step-by-step training I give them, but I've added other modules, as well as my new system of reading moods, to make this book "the advanced course." These additional pieces address the interplay between body language and emotions, how to use gestures and posture as tools in business and personal relationships, and tricks to remain inscrutable by controlling how and when your own body language leaks emotions.

Take a minute and refer to the flow chart provided on page 13. I want to give you a narrative guide to it as a complement, so that you understand at the outset how the information in the book helps you build the skill of reading body language. In other words, if you skip around, you'll pick up some hot tricks, but you can't become adept at reading body language by taking that approach.

Beginning with some notes about communication of all beings, I move to distinctly human communication. The next topic figures prominently in my course on reading body language: culture. In this section, I look at the human groupings that have a profound impact on the way we express ourselves. You *cannot* hope to read body language well unless you take culture into consideration. Next, I move to person-to-person similarities, and then person-to-person differences. After that, you can start to answer the question: What are the differences between a person in a normal state—a state of congruence between gestures and voice—and a person in the state of sending verbal messages that conflict with non-verbal messages? At this point, the focus goes to the individual.

What is normal for a particular person? What is abnormal for a particular person? Those questions put us at the narrowest part of the diagram. From there, I start moving back toward a broader perspective. Exercises in applying the skill begin with a look at celebrities, who give us a common point of focus. You know the players; you see them every day on television. That sets the stage for reading the body language of individuals around you, for understanding their motivation and drive in context. As you practice overlaying the culture in your developing picture of what's happening, you can begin to employ the skill in one-on-one business and personal relationships, and then expanding the application of your expertise to groups.

Over time, your self-awareness of body language evolves as you review, evaluate, analyze, and decide what other people are doing. At that point, you've progressed to a level of knowledge and control that gives you powerful advantages over most other people in your daily life.

What the pros know: TV vs. reality

The ability of television cops and lawyers to catch a killer seems almost magical. For them, clues glow in the dark and fall out of the rafters. And when they interview a suspect, they read his body language to confirm his guilt. Given the advantage of close-ups, and a director explaining when and how to mimic a behavior, you get to see what tips off the brilliant detective—but you don't necessarily know what it means. Rubbing the legs while he's talking (stress relief through energy displacement), pupils narrowing to a pinpoint when he sees a photo of the victim (the picture brings back the rage that led him to kill the guy who stole his money), and dry mouth (another sign of intense anger), all fit together for the smart cop, but all you perceive is a feeling that the suspect is an emotional wreck. These actors are, of course, working from a script, so they know the subtext, which the writer may or may not have gotten right. The truth is often much more subtle and difficult to read. Human subroutines can become really complex, and it is a rare combination of talent and experience that enables the writer-director-actor team to get it right.

Law & Order: Criminal Intent and *The Closer* provide great examples of the substantial information that a body-language expert can glean from interaction with a person. In the former, Vincent D'Onofrio stars as Detective Robert Goren, whom TV.com aptly describes as "an exceptionally bright homicide investigator with well-honed instincts that match up favorably with his criminal quarry." That's an eloquent way of saying that he does things almost no investigator outside of TV drama could pull off.

In an episode in which the killer is a method actor immersing himself in the role of a serial killer, D'Onofrio doesn't just read body language, he manipulates it to exploit the interplay between body posture and emotions. Casually questioning the suspect in his own home, Detective Goren tilts his head markedly to the left. The man gives a natural response—without being aware that he is mirroring the detective's action—tilting his head to the right. We look hard right and lean our head hard right as both a reflection and expression of emotion. Look at people at a funeral. Their eyes will be down and to the right, and sometimes the entire head is drooping to the right. Although some clinical psychologists have disagreed with me that this is possible, I have observed that "forcing" emotional body language through this mirroring technique actually pulls a person into an emotional state. This is what Goren did with his suspect. The man's responsive body language helped put him into an emotional state that made him vulnerable—and ready to confess.

My students have seen shows similar to this and think they've picked up lots of tricks. Because my students, who are aspiring interrogators in both the military and civilian sectors, have been hand-picked for my body language class, they come through the door embracing a paradox of their own creation: I'm good enough to be in this class, so I must already know most of what Hartley's going to teach me. (The ones who know I have a book out on the subject have a little more humility. The ones who've also researched what I've said are a little more cocky.)

I ask them what they know.

They often reference John Travolta's 2003 movie *Basic*, which "taught" them that a person looking up and to his right means he's lying; I tell them that they've been deceived. A broad conclusion such as this about a particular piece of body language usually has very little meaning. Until they are connected with other factors, and until you have baselined a person to determine what is normal behavior, you can't draw a conclusion about truth or deception based on a single eye movement. If you want to "read someone like a book," you need to look at the entire text and not just the section titles.

Another common misconception is that crossed arms always signify a barrier, a defensive gesture to block someone out, primarily because of insecurity. This gesture alone means nothing, and to make my point to students I cross my arms, furrow my brow, point to the person with my head, and overly enunciate the words, "Do I seem insecure to you?" This gets a chuckle from the students I didn't pick on, but my "victim" shuffles. He shifts in the chair, breaks eye contact, and laughs nervously; he may even blush. Do you recognize this body language? Yep, it's embarrassment.

Some of the other mistaken beliefs even come from "expert" sources writing about human patterns of behavior. They see a phrase such as "73 percent of the time, a man with his fingers in a steepling position is feeling self-confident" and conclude that the theory applies to all steepling—up, down, or sideways. Not so, as you will soon find out.

I think that using percentages similar to this to justify a conclusion about human behavior borders on nonsense. To me, assigning numbers to behavior patterns is an attempt to mask uncertainty. Humans are easily represented on a bell curve for any demographic. The greatest percentage is going to fall somewhere near the center with extreme deviations lying near the edges. This works for intelligence, skin tone, how white your teeth are, and how many times you have skinned your knee. It is not magic; it is simple math.

Even after these folks go through the basic body language course, they often allow their projections to contaminate what they observe. The turning point tends to be their failure to pinpoint the bad guy in a scenario that serves as a kind of final exam.

Right now, I'm going to give you one of those scenarios. If you determine what kind of body language the terrorist would have, then you are on the road to expertise in this field.

The scenario

You and two other people in your unit are sent to a farmhouse in northern Iraq. You have been told that an informant alleges that someone in that house is an IED (improvised explosive device) kingpin. You have room for only one person in your transport besides yourself, so you must find the individual that is most likely to be that person. In addition, you know that this person is known as Abulhul, or "father of despair." That's what the Sphinx is called in Egyptian, by the way.

You and your buddies kick the door in and find five people in the room having dinner—a middle-aged Iraqi male and two Iraqi couples. Everyone in the house appears to be Iraqi because of their physical appearance and clothing; everyone speaks an Iraqi dialect. At this point, you have one hour to determine who the terrorist is and get that person back to your unit.

You ask one of the men, who has a noticeable scar across his forehead: "What do you do for a living?"

"I sell timers and radios," he replies. He wrings his hands and rubs his head. Have you struck gold immediately?

His cousin, one of the other men in the room, admits to being an electronics repairman. "Don't listen to that stupid man," he says. He explains that his cousin suffered a serious head injury and functions only on a marginal level. He has trouble remembering words; instead of saying clocks, he said timers. "I try to help him," the man says, "by giving him clocks and radios that I repair to sell."

Suspicion now moves to the electronics repairman. You keep an eye on him, as he taps his fingers on the table and shifts in his chair. He clearly resents your presence, but says nothing.

You watch him out of the corner of your eye as you question his wife. She appears to be a simple woman who gives straightforward answers to questions, but clearly hates Americans.

With nowhere to go during the day, she sits home and watches television with her kids around the clock. The farmhouse is equipped with satellite TV, so she not only gets news, but also American crime shows, and a plethora of programs that cause her to conclude that the United States has a population of immoral, insane people. She spits at you and the other soldiers, as her husband gestures for her to sit down and shut up.

The electronics repairman's brother owns the house; he's a sheep farmer who makes a point that he has a thriving business. He uses his arms to indicate that his flock is enormous and that they keep him busy night and day. His wife has two kids at home and, similar to her sister-in-law, all she does is take care of the kids all day. From the way she answers questions, she seems to be more educated than the other woman.

After you ask a barrage of standard questions, such as "Where you were born? How long have you lived here?" the tactic you and your buddies use is to ask questions designed to make each person leak information about the others. You go after the woman who is vocal in her anti-Americanism and suggest she's obviously alone in her feeling.

"No!" she screams and points again and again to her sister-in-law. "Ask her. She knows what they're like!"

The other woman strides from where she was standing and faces you directly. "Yes, I know because I saw for myself how you kill," she says quietly. "She sees it only on TV."

The answer revealed

The students who figure out who the guilty party generally do so through questioning and by putting aside their preconceived notion that "father of despair" must be a man. Good questioning of the woman who hates Americans will reveal that she does not like or trust her sister-in-law, whom she does not consider a real Iraqi. Why? The wife of the shepherd left Iraq when she was 10 because her father was on the outs with the Saddam regime. Her family lived in Germany until after the first Gulf War, and then came back, thinking that the Shi'ites would take power.

A star student of body language will notice three telling things. First the wife of the electronics repairman points at the other woman in an accusing way as she says, "Ask her!" Second, the other woman moves in a way that suggests she has only recently started wearing Iraqi garb again. A woman who had worn pants for period of time would stride, but not a woman who has worn a dress and lived among traditional Iraqi women her whole life. Third, the shepherd's wife approached her questioner directly, which is uncharacteristic behavior. She has a Western woman's sense of comfort talking face-to-face with a man.

The truth you needed is this: She still has friends in Germany and mules sensitive information back and forth. She is the source of sophisticated design information and supplies for new IEDs.

The moral of the story is: Don't jump to conclusions based on things you think are true. Watch and listen for clues that add up logically, not ones that fit a pattern you think should be there.

One of the photos I show to provoke class analysis invariably gets the same reaction. The photo captures the face of women in babushkas. The students uniformly respond with descriptors, such as "weak," "frail," and "helpless." I remind them of the so-called Black Widows, Olga Rutterschmidt and Helen Golay—73 and 75, respectively, when they were captured in 2006—who murdered homeless men as part of their insurance scams. I find this to be a cultural bias. In a culture that values youth and vigor, the old cannot possibly be dangerous. Most Americans never consider what they would think if they met a 65-year-old Harrison Ford who didn't have the benefit of makeup and a good camera angle. Is he still Indiana Jones, or is he suddenly Professor Henry Jones?

Sheikh Omar Abdel-Rahman, who is now serving a life sentence at the Federal Administrative Maximum Penitentiary hospital in Colorado, is a blind Muslim cleric. Linked to the 1993 World Trade Center bombing, among other heinous acts, he may have looked pathetic, but his fatwa calling for violence again U.S. civilian targets made a powerful terrorist.

What I teach the pros

Communication

I break human communication into three channels:

⇒ Verbal: Word choice.

⇒ Vocal: All human voice components that do not include word choice.

⇒ Non-verbal: All other pieces of communication.

I think of the verbal as the servant of the will; it is the easiest channel to control. People can more easily select their words than they can control their nervous coughs or eye tics. Think about how much more powerful your communication becomes as you increase your level of control over the other two as well.

There's no doubt that you've had exposure to someone so well-spoken that simply hearing him or her inspires you. When I was a young soldier, I worked for a lieutenant with this gift; he thoroughly impressed me until I realized he was speaking at half the speed of everyone else. That gave him time to choose each word carefully. Great speakers not only make precise word choices, but they control cadence, similar to the lieutenant, as well as tone, pitch, and a host of utterances that are part of the vocal component of communication.

The third channel—non-verbal—includes gesturing, posture, proximity to others, and other factors explored throughout this book. A premise of the approach I teach is that, in terms of non-verbal communication, there are fewer differences than similarities among people, otherwise we couldn't communicate as a species.

I start every class with a definition of communication that is straight from *Merriam-Webster*: "A process by which information is exchanged between individuals through a common system of symbols, signs, or behavior." While your brain may focus on the last part of the definition—symbols, signs, or behavior—I want to call your attention to a couple of words that precede it, namely, "process" and "system." Process is what occurs between the beginning and the end. It implies causality. System describes independent parts coming together into an organized whole. For example, rage may be sparked by a thought, but the communication of it is the process that includes a balled fist, an arm that goes rigid, contracting pupils, a rigid back, and so on. The end point may be the enraged person planting his knuckles on some other guy's jaw. This rage can be communicated without intent, too, as long as you know the sequence of body movements that effectively convey it. A good interrogator has the capacity to communicate rage where there is none, just as a good actor does. Although many interrogators believe that this is the most difficult emotion to portray, I don't because few people have ever seen true rage.

Therefore, given that communication means a bit more than a single grunt or foot stomp, a typical first question from students is, "Do animals communicate?"

The simple answer is yes. Cats, dogs, horses, goldfish, hamsters, and monkeys all have a system of symbols and behavior that convey information. I want to draw a distinction here between those actions that take shape as communication and simple, non-verbal behavior. When a cat scratches her ear, she isn't trying to tell you anything; she's scratching because her ear itches. Keep this distinction in mind for humans behavior, too. Sometimes a scratch is just that.

The difference between animal communication and human communication is, of course, complexity. Our pets generally communicate in a series of utterances, shifts in posture, flexing of extremities, and eye movement. The most mentally advanced of these animals, the primate, has monkeys on the low end of the spectrum and great apes toward the high end. Beyond them, sitting at the tip of this communication chain, is the greatest of apes: human beings.

Often when I teach or deliver a presentation, I get people who reject evolution, so they challenge me: "So you believe we descended from monkeys?"

I say, "No. We *are* monkeys—really fancy ones." I often call humans the shaved ape, which is a take-off on Desmond Morris's *The Naked Ape*. I think we are not "naked," as much as "shaved," meaning that we try very hard to remove the animal from who we are.

A version of another question usually comes up after that: "Is human language an effective system of symbols? Most of my students instantly say yes. My answer: no.

A very effective system of symbols would be one that conveyed our thoughts precisely. Even with the most astute communicators, spoken English can be confusing.

No reading aloud.

No reading allowed.

Homonyms, multiple meaning of words and connotations that overtake the denotations of words (for example, terrific) all make English a tough language to learn. The French Academy makes rules to avert this kind of mess; we in the United States seem to enjoy the creative exercise of fostering the mess.

Read this question aloud: *Would you prefer to lie?*

What is the meaning? It could be an accusation, or asking about a choice of relaxation. Whether in print or spoken, you cannot tell. Should you be insulted if a person says this to you? Maybe you look tired and don't know it. How much of the meaning comes through in the spoken words? How much of the meaning would the speaker convey through body language? Would a slight drop of the brow or scowl of the lips help you to understand? How about tone and inflection? Emphasis on "you" carries a different sense from an emphasis on "prefer." How much do you think an accent or pronunciation would affect comprehension of the meaning if you simply heard the sentence on the radio?

Akin to our chimp cousins, we convey information on many channels, and although we prefer to think of ourselves as so much more, we respond to these signals as readily as our chimp cousins. It means that someone who better understands the cues and meanings can control the conversation in a way even Machiavelli himself, with his humanist beliefs, could not imagine.

By missing the animal piece of communication—shrieks, limbs flailing, eyes darting, and arched back—we reduce our ability to comprehend. No language alone can reach the subtlety of spoken language overlaid on effective non-verbal communication.

Body movement

The next question I ask in class that guides me to my step-by-step instruction is: Who understands body language? I then move very close to the desk of one of the people who does not raise his or her hand and stare menacingly at that student. As the class laughs, the person usually raises his hand. The point is made: We all understand body language on *some* level; most people simply do not pay attention to the subtle pieces of daily communication. Many people can see body language on a subconscious level, but they override their perceptions. We are taught to "be logical," as if there were such a thing as logic when dealing with most humans.

As I mentioned previously, I go from verbal to vocal to non-verbal communication, with the latter two receiving primary focus, because reading those is the real meat of the subject, or something my fellow interrogators often call "voodoo," that is, reading the unintentional cues presented by the source. In other words, what is the other person telling me that he really does not want me to know?

After we move through the body-language curriculum, I give my students the offensive applications, or how to influence someone gently into what you want. A long-time colleague of mine calls this "interrogator mind tricks," an obvious reference to George Lucas's inflated version of this, the Jedi mind tricks. The connection is intimate: I teach the ability to tap in on a subconscious level to a person's mind and get the response I want or need.

There's a systematic process behind this. I begin with baselining, and then move to body parts.

Baselining

Baselining is a portable version of the polygraph. You use it to pick up subtle variables in body language and tone of voice.

Once you know what to look and listen for, you can detect changes that accompany stress of varying degrees. That ability gives you a high degree of control in your interaction with someone.

Starting later in the book, I will emphasize the importance of observing the body language of an individual in a relaxed state, that is, seeing what happens naturally, without affectation or stress.

I will highlight what gestures and physical responses are involuntary and universal, because these are *not* what you focus on in baselining. You will take every other kind of gesture and physical response into consideration, however.

Body parts

In beginning the scan of body movements, I start with the face. To steal the words of Desmond Morris, the face is the organ of expression. Our agreement ends there. Morris conjectured that it is the easiest to control because it is the closest to the brain, but I strongly disagree. When it comes to the face, I think we're dealing with a paradox: The face is both the easiest and the hardest area of the body to control. There are many things we do with our faces that we aren't even aware of because they are second nature.

A lot of emotion comes out through the brow in both voluntary and involuntary expressions. We use the forehead muscles when we normally interact with people, even on the phone, and we develop wrinkles as a result. If Morris were right and we can control the muscles in the face more easily than others, then we wouldn't be using so much Botox. We could voluntarily stop using the muscles that create the problem, and even voluntarily reverse the process of wrinkling by exercising them. In addition, if the face were under our control, more facial movements would be cultural, not universal.

Facial movements become practiced behavior over time, because we learn how to present an even smile when meeting someone and an arched eyebrow when our kid drops mustard on the floor. But the plethora of muscles in our faces makes it hard for us to keep track of them. We often do not even realize the range of emotions and physiological reactions we express with our faces. What does that upturned brow mean? Is there a difference if the person sending the message is male or female? If the receiver is male or female? How do the sexes differ in messaging, not only with the same sex but the opposite sex? Is that well-intended signal misread because of differences in the two brains? The head is the workhorse of communication. And although much of what it conveys is intentional, we still leak messages that are impossible to cover.

From the head, face, and neck, I move to the arms, and then down to through the rest of the body: hands and gesturing, torso, legs, and feet. Do those folded arms really mean the person is guarded and maybe even disgusted? Do those crossed feet indicate you are shutting me out? This is where people's absolutes start to break down, because they learn that you can't draw conclusions without understanding context.

Context

At first, my students fight the premise that context has huge significance in reading body language. "John Travolta didn't need context to figure out the guy was lying...." The assumption they embrace is that an involuntary movement can be understood out of context, for example, pupil movement. The pupils enlarge to take in more information and contract to block it out.

That action does give you a clue about the person's emotional state, but without context you will not know if the pupils dilated because of sexual arousal or fear, or if they narrowed to pinpoints because of disgust.

Context contains a number of elements in addition to gestures and facial expressions, such as space, time, and even smell.

What to expect

At the end of the session on reading body language, my students look at everyone differently. From their prisoners or employees to their in-laws, they have a more intelligent understanding of what the other chimps are saying to them.

They, and now you, will look at newsreels of Adolf Hitler's wild, flailing arms and see something that his desperate followers did not. You will understand why, years after his insane despotry, many people still call him a communications genius; you will perceive the mechanisms that allowed him to be effective. You will also see gestures that bleed sickness.

You will regain something your primitive ancestors used daily: a second sight to body language.

Culture: The Big External Influence

Ruthless Celtic kings and their chiefs had body language that defined them. A nasty, belching bunch, they could easily be identified by "hands twitching to the sword hilt at the imagined hint of an insult...wiping the greasy moustaches that were a mark of nobility," in the words of anthropologist Stuart Piggott in *Ancient Europe* (Edinburgh: The University Press, 1965, p. 229).

This is a description that highlights features of the Celtic warriors' culture, but every culture has the same binding elements: beliefs, traditions, behaviors, and rules. These elements work together to engender security within the group and keep people riding in the same direction. In its most primitive sense, culture separated one group of apes from another group of apes; it enabled them to know whom to tolerate and whom to destroy.

Culture is nothing more than accepted social norms for a group. How do these norms come about? Do groups get together and vote, or do they simply adopt precedent-setting moves? The answer is somewhere in between because cultures can arise from small sub-groups, or microcultures, all the way up to humankind. In terms of our study of body language, the concept of microcultures includes couples: male-female, female-female, or male-male. Every group has created norms for what is acceptable. More importantly, every microculture has created taboos as well. Cultures that reach across humankind become what I call a super-culture. With modern media saturation and global product marketing, gestures, words, and even attitudes can become super-cultural. The words "okay" and "Coca-Cola" are the two most recognized in the world.

Culture affects every aspect of understanding body language. It affects how people move, even resulting in fine distinctions between many so-called universal, involuntary movements, such as raising eyebrows when you recognize another person. It also affects how you perceive the message associated with another person's body language. Your filters rooted in prejudices of different kinds and the way you project meaning took shape as a result of your culture.

I use a simple model to depict where someone fits within a culture: the bell curve. The first thing to remember in moving a person onto the bell curve is that he may be part of many cultures or microcultures. Similar to members of the Old South's Ku Klux Klan, who covered their identities in white sheets, we all carry around ties to microcultures that are not evident when we are grouped with the mass. You will start sorting behavior as cultural, super-cultural, or sub-cultural on a model where the "cultural" refers to the greater group of which you are part. You will routinely start placing individuals and behaviors on bell curves.

The bell curve represents a range of values. I use this example in class: How many have had a skinned knee at least once? Everyone raises his hand. Twice? Most keep a hand up. Five times? Only a few hands remain. The bell curve based on that information looks similar to this, and I've added the terms sub-typical, typical, and super-typical to clarify the concept.

In this model anyone with a skinned knee less than twice is sub-typical, two to five times becomes the norm, and more than five times is super-typical. Is this a distorted view of the group? Sure, but it does represent one aspect of the group dynamic. It also gives us a model for further analyzing the meaning of the data and targeting something about this group to understand the group's identity. People seize on differences to create taboos and create a culture. We can overlay this into a more normal everyday situation.

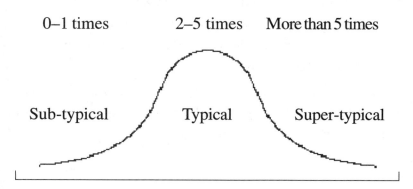

0–1 times   2–5 times   More than 5 times

Sub-typical   Typical   Super-typical

Examples:

1. Bill Gates is super-typical in the greater understanding of American culture. A healthy 25-year-old man who lives with, and is supported by his parents is sub-typical. A 40-year-old woman who works in the human resources department of a manufacturing company is typical. Are there aspects of American culture in which Bill Gates is sub-typical or labeled as a geek? Sure. This helps us to better understand why demographics and statistics can be used to make any point we want to make.

2. Within a high school group, you can easily spot the kids who are the most admired. These super-typical kids may be the athletes, cheerleaders, or student council leaders, depending on the school. Next are the masses, or the typical. In this group are the normal kids with average social skills who do not stand out among the others. Kids with poor social skills populate the last group; this may include the gangly kid who is not comfortable with his quickly growing body. These kids are the sub-typical. The students call them names, such as "the bean" and "stick man" to remind them of this status.

In this model the super-typical have sway over the typical, who, in turn, disregard the sub-typical. They tolerate the sub-typical as part of the greater group, but given the opportunity to separate, the typical would group with the super-typical. If this is not an option, they may fragment within their own group into other microcultures. The typical admire and even emulate the super-typical in the hope of gaining their approval. The sub-typical hope to become typical.

Consider this example before you dismiss this view as too simplistic. In the early 1970s, a researcher from the State University of New York (SUNY) interviewed children of migrant farm workers. "What do you want to be when you grow up?" she asked. When encouraged to lift up their imaginations and hopes, most of the kids said, "Crew foreman." Very few named professions, such as a doctor or lawyer.

Our primate cousins behave this way. The super-typical comprise the ruling class of chimps. The alpha-male establishes a pecking order in which he is king. All others jockey for position. The pack includes the super-typical, alpha-male and female, the masses, and the sub-typical, but the last group is barely part of the pack. Humankind repeats this model on different scales.

Do we emulate the super-typical in our subculture? Look around you at your workplace. Do you emulate the behavior of the alpha-female or male in hope of approval? Does the latest trend started by super-typical Celebrity X spark spin-offs in the population? Even if you think you are immune, would you ever comment on a fact related to a celebrity, for example, that Britney Spears was caught driving with her baby on her lap? Celebrity watching has grown into a billion-dollar industry, serving the intellectual curiosity of a nation of pop culture geniuses. How typical.

By addressing this topic of culture up front, I want to arouse your awareness of how imperative it is that you ask yourself, "How important is it that I'm American or Japanese when trying to read that person's body language?" "How much do my Islamic or Jewish beliefs affect my perception of the meaning of her gestures?" "How much does the fact that I'm a staunch Republican or a devoted Communist color my understanding of his presentation?" And, as corollaries, you will ask questions such as, "Am I a typical Republican?" and "Is she a typical American?"

Ape culture is simple. Big alpha-male dominates; paired with alpha-female, he becomes the ruling hierarchy. Other male apes may scheme and attempt to breed part of the harem without the knowledge of the alpha-male, but alphas absolutely control social norming. At one point in our development, human culture was likely very similar to the super-typical—clearly defined.

Looking back at the Celtic chieftain I mentioned in the opening of this chapter, we can see a more sophisticated model in his culture than in the ape world. The king and his sub-chiefs were the super-typical. Going against the rules—publicized by word of mouth and personal observation—resulted in retribution. In their shaved-ape world, king and chieftains became the alpha-chimps. Consistent with their primate nature, people recognized the super-typical and began to emulate.

On the rare occasions when a "superior" member of the clan copied behavior of someone with less stature, he wanted something and determined that the copied behavior would get it for him. It could have been a style of socializing or the choice of person he took to bed.

This pattern continued to evolve throughout the ages until reaching our modern era. Looking for the super-typical, people often found them in clergy, politicians, and the wealthy. This happened for obvious reasons: The average man had no voice outside his immediate sub-group, and no means to amplify his voice. In fact, he didn't even know the words to amplify, which is why the literate clergy represented a ruling class of its own. The wealthy achieved that status through connections, and belonged to an established structure with implied power.

As media has proliferated and communication has become ubiquitous, these relationships have taken a dramatic turn. Briefly, I want to explore American culture with you as a way of understanding how cultures evolve—and preparing you to make the intimate link between the resultant culture and body language.

Even within a culture generally described as "American," there are divisions you need to consider, to ask yourself how typical, super-typical, or sub-typical you are within those. In the United States, for example, a big part of our culture is a sense of entitlement.

From its inception, the American culture espoused a belief that all men are created equal. Although often not as valid in practice as in theory, it was an American ideal. At that time, few people had the means or savvy to use media in presenting such ideas across the colonies. Enough of them held a belief that the fledgling country needed to allow common people an opportunity to succeed—so the message hit the streets.

With its independence, the United States established a unique culture that consisted of disparate groups, each of which assimilated in its own way. We have often referred to this as the melting pot. The melting-pot concept implies that, slowly as they cook in the fires of a national heat, the characteristics of "typical" change based on the percentage of the population each group represents. Each person entering the country assimilates to his or her new home and decides exactly how to fit in.

Southern planters and Northern industrialists, each with their own distinct ideas about what it meant to be American, were the super-typical. These ideas were shared by enough of the respective population to lose more than 600,000 American lives during the war between the states. Do I believe that the super-typical merely ordered these people to fight? No. No more than I believe the average Southerners lived similarly to Scarlett O'Hara. These people had come to identify with very different pictures of what it meant to be American, and the Civil War was the occasion to reconcile those two pictures. This is hard-fought social norming.

As a result of this conflict, the freedman emerged as a new class of American citizen. Particularly in areas where they had been slaves, these people were treated as the sub-typical. The Americans who had gone to war and lost that war would vilify them and, in some cases, even deny them rights. Think of the chimp model again: A super-typical alpha who is dropped to typical status will become more than disdainful of the sub-typical. This would prove to be one of the most complex assimilations in American history.

Here is what's going on behind the curtain: As a result of a melting-pot culture, some sub-groups lie outside cultural norms. These people should enjoy the rights of the greater culture, but don't. The nature of humans is to deny those who are not the typical or super-typical as much as possible. The sub-typical receive different treatment from the typical or super-typical.

The super-typical people of the day, principally politicians and activists, tried to correct these wrongs through writings and speeches. Which do you think carried the most power, even in an age before mass-media? Imagine the presence of a 6-foot, 5-inch tall Abraham Lincoln delivering the Gettysburg Address. By visual contact and word-of-mouth, Lincoln rose to the throne of alpha-chimp.

After this, American culture expanded steadily to include large groups of Mexican immigrants, Pacific Islanders, Inuit, and many others. Assimilation can be painful, especially for those assimilating. Each new group brought new flavors to the melting pot. Meanwhile, the belief that all men are created equal was tested.

The Great Depression hit America at the time of a fledgling technology: radio. A new kind of American politician evolved:

the media-savvy politician. Now, not only the verbal, but also the vocal portion of a president's speech could be experienced first-hand.

This time of "doing without" for Americans offered fertile ground for President Franklin Delano Roosevelt when he came up with the New Deal and, through radio, spoke to average Americans in their own homes about entitlement. Could anyone become more super-typical than a president with a plan for *you* in your own living room? Without an image of FDR in the wheelchair, Americans heard only his message. Still, photos provided the only source of body language to most people. He was the alpha in our living rooms telling Americans how much they deserved—just for living. A new sense of entitlement flourished as the new media broadcasting the images became ubiquitous.

After Roosevelt held an omnipresent power with his voice, John F. Kennedy held it with his face. He personally, but also through the legacy of his presidency, engendered a lively sense of entitlement. Is there any doubt as to why Americans were inconsolable when they watched their quintessential alpha die at the hands of some nondescript upstart one fall afternoon? This nation with the perception of super power had its most alpha male destroyed by a sub-typical hiding in a storage room. Such ignominy was inconceivable. I believe it is the reason why JFK's death still fuels the greatest conspiracy theories in the United States today.

Returning to the historical context, people who endured sustained denial of the basic rights of the typical, as well as their supporters, got angry. The United States began to develop a conscience and a culture that recognized this.

Enter media powered by new technologies. They offered the super-typical an opportunity to redress in ways FDR's generation could not imagine.

African-Americans, members of the sub-typical, had little access. But there were super-typical, as well as African-Americans, who had both drive and access, and a conscience to stand with the sub-typical. Their efforts launched the Civil Rights movement, and the course was set to create a culture that tolerated differences in the framework of equal rights under the law.

And then came an ideological hijacking. More media translated into more media access by more people. Americans could become super-typical simply by being on camera or in print. It is impossible to sustain an identity based on standing in front of the camera when the camera makes every part of a person's life a subject for coverage. Even if he could maintain this status, it is much more desirable to become super-typical in a subculture of the sub-typical.

These new super-typical citizens understood that they needed causes to maintain their identity. A common way to forge it was by spotlighting areas where their sub-typical neighbors struggled, by raising the flag of entitlement as it pertained to food, healthcare, or education, for example. Others who became super-typical due to their talent (including a "talent," such as inherited wealth), were seduced by their own image. But unlike Narcissus admiring his own reflection in the pool, much of the population joined them in the love fest. Who could blame these celebrities for developing a sense of superiority in multiple aspects of life? Through precedent, people gave them the right to display that superiority by advising the ordinary people in matters of lifestyle, domestic politics, and even international relations. They, too, saw the need to adopt causes to maintain their identity.

This situation, in which celebrities with a range of mental abilities and wisdom make pronouncements on social change, results in three outcomes:

1.   It helps a culture of victims to take shape.

2.   It further raises the celebrity status of those super-typical people who have exhibited righteous indignation over the treatment of the sub-typical.

3.   The concept of tolerance assumes a distorted meaning: "whatever." As in, "do whatever you want," and "be whatever you want."

When something such as this happens, no one aspires to become the typical. Remember the bell curve? People in a culture with these pressures now aspire to the super-typical *only*—they want to be super-typical in their *own* microculture, whatever that is—and they contort their behavior to get there. They hang on to anything that makes them special, that distinguishes them as unique.

Voilá! The result is America is a jellybean jar, rather than a melting pot. Create more celebrity by being different, and in the process, sacrifice "American culture" by glorifying uniqueness. The paradox that also affects thinking and behavior, of course, is that

"American culture" affords rights and privileges based on the ideology that we are all created equal.

We keep circling back to the discussion of entitlement. Most of us feel we have a right to the basics, not only of survival, but a quality of life. We have a right to personal mobility and choices at the grocery store. We have the right of appeal if a court case doesn't go our way. And in many peoples' minds, we have the right to yell profanities at a politician, preacher, or police officer we hate. Depending on who we are, that sense of entitlement can have vastly different implications, and others in the world might view some of them as bizarre, even though Americans are not alone in feeling this is a right. (Remember the 2005 youth riots in France over the entitlement not to be fired from a job?) Combine the concepts of "subjugated" with "born with a spectrum of rights," and the result is a super-entitled victim.

When we go overseas, we are often lumped together as "the ugly American," because people abroad recognize our sense of entitlement and may make a sweeping assumption about how it affects our gestures and language. They don't necessarily take into consideration that, depending on how strong the sense of entitlement is, an American's reaction to a violation can range from the obvious to the subtle, from purposeful affectations to movements emanating from the subconscious.

Probably more than any other cultural group, Americans suffer from culture shock when traveling abroad due to perceived homogeneity of the entire North American continent. Most Americans from Monterey to Manhattan share at least a common language and jargon for finding what they need. When this does not work, there is a huge displacement of expectations.

Most Americans expect to walk into a government office in the United States and get an answer in English. Is this a reasonable expectation? Today, yes. In times to come, when the majority of the jellybeans do not speak English as a first language, maybe not.

A hard-won homogeneity of culture in the United States will disappear as the predominately Germanic culture dies off. Speculate about a time when Americans are primarily Hispanic and the typical becomes a Spanish speaker. Then what happens to new immigrants from other regions of the world? The jellybean jar changes labels to the Spanish equivalent and the new ethnic group feels victimized until either every sign in every building is in their language, too, or the new Hispanic typical says, "Learn the language of the land." This sense of entitlement is not free. Who pays for the interpreters?

The days have passed when Americans identified with singular role models, such as John Wayne. Modern heroes tend to be big names in their microcultures—skateboarder, rock star, tattoo artist—and we look to media and advertising that feature them for our cultural norming. With the proliferation of media, every microculture can have its own spokesperson (super-typical) on the air. Becoming similar to those people validates our attempts to be unique; we no longer see them as an outcast. Because the super-typical "must" be right, their image is the image of what it means to be American, not only to us, but also to the rest of the world as well. Arabs in Iraq watch the Brady Bunch—I know this for a fact and have also heard it from Army buddies who have served there in the most recent war. Imagine how repeated exposure to the Brady kids' sibling rivalry and family vacations in Hawaii affects how Iraqis view Americans. No wonder they're a little surprised when someone who looks like Peter Brady comes to their door with an M16 strapped to him.

Now, let's move to the influence of super-typical on the typical, but on a smaller scale.

One factor that contributes to the different forms of response is the influences of sub-groups within a culture. Why are Texans seen as brash by other fellow Americans even though we're all part of the "same culture"? Their heritage and accomplishments shape behavior patterns. Texans carved an environment in the wilderness from nothing, rounding up their cattle and introducing organization where there was none. They claim the distinction of being the only American state to ever be an independent nation. The super-typicals of Texas, such as Stephen Austin, Sam Houston, Davy Crockett, and Jim Bowie earned larger-than-life status. So Texans have an ingrained pride about being tough; they are a force to be reckoned with and traditionally have a fierce sense of entitlement. Add to that the fact that many of the original immigrants were Germans, who have a guttural language that people from

Latin-language areas hear as harsh. So, how did people with a contrasting background, say, East Coast English, tend to describe Texans? They strutted. They were loud. Their gestures were too big. This became the heritage of the modern Texan. Just as the mentality of the Old South affects the psyche of the modern Southern child, or like the magnitude of the 9/11 attacks on the World Trade Center will affect generations of New Yorkers, so too does the larger-than-life Texan affects a child of the Lone Star State. Though much of the old culture is gone, it is still echoed in the behavior of people who call themselves Texans.

Almost invariably, you will observe distinctive body language associated with a group, as large as Texas or as small as a high-school cheerleading squad. Even temporary groups, such as a fraternity pledge class, a clique of pot-smoking kids at school, a street gang, or a team of gung-ho salesmen will create unique "tribal customs." Sean Hayes's prancing, limp-wristed portrayal of Jack McFarland on *Will & Grace* established him as a proud member of the social group known as "gay men who don't even remember where the closet is anymore." In contrast, a lot of gestures common within foreign cultures may go unnoticed by us or may arouse an inappropriate reaction because we have no idea what it really means. These cultural norms are direct responses to social pressure, both positive and negative. While the super-typical may get away with introducing something new, an average Joe will be chastised for the attempt. Similar to the alpha-chimp, human societies have a way of forcing compliance.

Rites of passage and social norming

Although associated with particular cultures, people in the culture may or may not even acknowledge that certain common practices fall into the "rites of passage" category. Rites of passage are connected with body language because they affect how a culture evolves.

Passing a driver's test is a rite of passage in the United States. Soon after that, the urge to walk simply to get someplace often subsides. It is rare for Americans to walk on a regular basis unless they're city dwellers. Does this show in our body language? Absolutely.

Consider how all of the following extreme examples affect the body language, temporary or even permanently, of the people who have experienced them:

⇒ **Sunna circumcision:** An Arab practice, reflecting what some perceive as consistent with Islamic law and tradition, that removes part of the clitoris. Because it is usually performed on adult women, it can have a profound effect on self-image and, therefore, behavior. By the way, I can't even remember the astonishing number of my students—many of whom are about to be deployed to regions of the Middle East—who say, "Aww, they don't do that anymore."

Guess again. Now consider the impact of this imposed ritual on a young woman if she were the only one in the village having *not* been through this?

⇛ **Pederasty:** In terms of ritual, we commonly associate this practice of adult men introducing young boys to sex as a Greek institution, but many other cultures have practiced it as well. I don't mean to imply that the practice has died, either.

⇛ **Scarification:** Whether it's done by cutting or burning, this is a ceremonial injuring of a person in such a way that the scar tissue forms a particular design. Depending on the culture, it could mark the person as an adult male, a female who's ready and willing to bare children, a criminal, a part of a tribe, and so on.

⇛ **Starting to wear make-up and nail polish (without mom's help):** American girls definitely use this as a sign of being grown up, at least grown up enough to flirt. Using nail polish and make-up of their own choosing means that these girls think they're ready to make a few other decisions without their mother's help—and the body language shows it.

Everywhere around you, rites of passage occur daily and give rise to social norming. The effect of social norming is that, every time you repeat a ritual with a group, you become more cohesive with the group. These rites of passage traditionally occur at certain times in a person's assimilation with the group and can be formal or informal. If rites of passage are rushed, delayed, or forgone, the consequences can range from insignificant to dire. A son who lives with his parents until 25 and suddenly becomes famous may have minor repercussions as an adult, while the child whose sexual maturity is rushed because she's competing in beauty pageants at the age of 5 may well have a difficult adult life. Expectations—emotions that feed entitlements—will affect behavior.

In considering rites of passage, don't overlook any human interaction. Rites of passage are created to separate you from one group and bond you to another forever, changing the way you think. They may be elaborate and codified or spur of the moment. From circumcision to baptism to your first pair of bifocals, each has an effect forever on the way you perceive yourself. They summon the sub-typical chimp to emulate the alpha.

At an early age, American boys learn restroom etiquette as they observe dad, big brother, or uncle behaving "like a man" in the restroom. (For many young boys, the rite of passage underlying this is that they finally get to go to the restroom with dad instead of mom.) This behavior relates closely to rituals similar to the secret handshake of the Freemasons: every time a person participates in some activity, it leaves residual memory. In some cases, it even becomes muscle memory, because done enough times, the action becomes involuntary.

Exercise

Make a short list of formal cultural norming practices in place around you that affect how you behave. A few examples are:

⇒ If you attend a church with services dominated by ritual (the Catholic Mass, for instance), what behaviors are required of you? Do any of those behaviors surface when you're around the same people, even in a setting outside of church?

⇒ The Medieval re-creations (in which I'm very involved) require strict adherence to certain courtly and battle-field practices. A deviation from that will likely get you booted out of the group, or publicly chastised.

Here's another thought to get you started: I know of a 30-person company that adopted a no smoking policy in the workplace in the early 1990s, before it was a common practice. All six smokers who worked there eventually found themselves taking breaks about the same time and hanging out at the same spot outside the building. They grew into their own sub-culture within the organization and established social norming practices such as when and where to take breaks, body language to signal "it's time to take a break," or "I wish it were time to take a break."

If you're part of five groups, you'll have social mimicry in all five of them, even ones as informal as the smokers' group. By the way, can you imagine the additional social pressure each one had to remain a smoker after years, or even a few months, of repeating this pattern Monday through Friday?

As this example shows, then, you can have very narrow social norms, as well as very broad ones, such as those associated with your service in the military or your national heritage (for example, you put your hand over your heart when you pledge allegiance to the flag).

These types of social norms and cultural rituals are an overlay for everyone who is alive. In reading body language, therefore, you absolutely have to consider them. Think in terms of what distinctive traits or marks you can identify based on how they identify each other.

In practicing your identification skills, pay attention to what people do at all kinds of events associated with a culture. Whether they are rites of passage, such as a wedding or funeral, or entertainment, they showcase ritual behavior of that culture. Weddings and funerals provide formal examples of how people in that group display love and grief as an overlay to the involuntary ways that all human beings express love and grief. Sporting events exhibit how people in a culture demonstrate support. Do they cheer and applaud their own team more than they boo and throw beer cans at the opponent? The differences are the basis for sub-cultural stereotypes such as "Phillies' fans" who seem to boo with their whole bodies. As for Hollywood culture, the Academy Awards are a good occasion to see how ritual is not always synchronous with an actor's real emotions. Most of the people on the red carpet try hard to behave in a stately manner and to accept their awards with dignity. You can see a lot of glitchy behavior in this crowd because they try to use rituals of the event to disguise their true feelings.

This norming criterion is also a good way to determine who is not part of a tribe. The guest at a funeral who's bored, and shows it, probably isn't a close member of the grieving family. The Phillies' fan who applauds when Barry Bonds hits a home run needs to leave town before he's run out of it. When you practice this evaluation, are you profiling?

Now that I've gone down that controversial path, I will tell you that you will think differently about other people if you absorb the lessons in this book and practice R.E.A.D. Depending on your level of adoption of these techniques, I am changing your social norms.

Exercise

Tell people you are reading a book on body language. See what they do. When they respond with some combination of curiosity and concern—and you read it—say, "They said you would do that." Keep watching, because the next response will be predictable, too!

As you do this, your own social norms are changing a little bit at a time.

The shock of a new culture

Culture is a way of connecting with our fellow chimps, and identifying the differences between us and them, when we run into a new breed of chimp. We have been conditioned from birth to behave in certain ways in response to stimulus, and our microcultures regulate that response, even from infancy. An alpha, parent or other, dominates that microculture.

Every time we react to stimulus and adopt new behaviors presented by a parent, we are adopting the culture of our family. This goes on with limited incursions from other bands of chimps. Then, one day, the inevitable happens. We come face to face with new chimps—similar to a baby sitter—and new cultural norms. In the case of a sitter, the new alpha is akin to a captor: things will return to normal when she leaves. We learn this quickly.

The most profound culture shock in a child's life is more likely daycare or the first day of school. Now this child must deal with a new person who is solidly alpha. He must adopt the ways of this alpha while in her presence. The food, the lighting, the blankets— suddenly the child's perception of his place in the hierarchy goes into a blender. To make it equally difficult, the child must retain an understanding of what the alpha in the nest wants. This is profound culture shock. Most people cannot remember it, but they certainly recognize it in their own children.

This same thing takes affect when you walk into a new office, new school, or new relationship. The difference, in most cases, is that you speak the same language, eat the same food, and have at least some gesturing and acceptable behaviors in common. You see and identify or become the new alpha, and the culture adapts.

Sometimes you get caught between cultures until you're really sure what all the "rules" of the new culture are. A great place to watch this cultural evolution is school, whether it's first grade or college. You utter sounds, wear clothes, add body adornments, and make gestures that attract those who want to attract. Some of the efforts are very much on the conscious level and some of them are not. Often, until you're sure who it is you want to attract—and this applies to people in whom you're interested sexually as well as people you want as non-sexual companions—you might send mixed messages. You wear the clothes of the type of people you aim to spend time with, but may not have captured their vocabulary or cadence of speech, for example.

Through this adaptation we all learn to be successful organisms within a culture, whether a microculture or super-culture. Exposure is the key. We adapt skills that work, and we orchestrate their use with other skills that we learn as we go. When we move to a new place and the skills no longer produce the desired result, we have no concept or location to store that information. We start to grasp for something that will work. The chimp in us wins. We instinctively know that emulating the alpha's behavior is better than not.

In *Rangers Lead the Way* (Adams Media, 2003), former U.S. Army Ranger Dean Hohl talks about the cultural differences among the newbies he entered training with, and how and why the Ranger culture submerged when they were on duty:

> The first day I got to my Ranger unit, I was with a group of people who were "home." Up until that point, I was in training, so I was always carrying my bags with me. I didn't have much in the way of personal clothing—maybe one pair of jeans and a T-shirt. But these guys who had been in the Ranger unit for so long had settled in and made a home, with clothing and other personal items. I looked around and there was a guy in a cowboy hat, another one in biker leathers, one guy looked like a preppie from back East, another had on a T-shirt picturing a heavy metal band, another guy came across as a hillbilly. They spent their off hours doing wildly different things. Socially, they didn't pretend to have anything in common. I was dumbfounded by the differences between them.
>
> Though these differences were sharp, they became irrelevant when we were on a mission. When we put on our Ranger uniform and beret and heard Captain Thomas say, "This is your objective," we were a team.
>
> Ranger training and culture. . .translate into patterns that are more focused on practical, measurable outcomes...

Because culture involves choice, a person can suddenly change his body language in response to culture shock. Part of the change may be mimicking what appears to be accepted gestures, and part of it may be subduing what comes naturally because it seems out of place. Take for instance the habit of crossing the legs to make yourself comfortable. Many American men cross legs in the figure-four style, that is, one leg crossing the other with the ankle or calf resting on the knee. Men from the Middle East would not assume this posture for two reasons. One is seating styles, and the other is that showing the soles of the feet is insulting. The pressure on an American man negotiating with Middle Eastern people would be to avoid that body posture and adopt something more appropriate for the context.

Culture shock results simply from moving from one culture to another. It commonly involves four stages:

1. Euphoria over being in a new environment.
2. Irritation that things are different.
3. Adaptation to the new culture, which is typically a process rather a quick transformation.
4. Full recovery/full adaptation.

Some of the adjustments that a culture-shocked traveler might make are the proximity at which you stand to someone, the amount of time you look into a stranger's eyes, and whether or not you sit with your legs crossed.

Because culture affects every part of our being, from cadence to how close we stand to people, the broader our understanding of other cultures, the less likely we are to suffer culture shock. The more exposed we are to new things, the fuller our repertoire of what is acceptable, or even normal. And as we age, we all compartmentalize and create specific strategies for adaptation.

Learning to R.E.A.D.
(Review Evaluate
Analyze Decide)

PART II

Review From Scalp to Soles: R of R.E.A.D.

To learn to read body language, you will use a piecemeal approach in the beginning, and then move to a holistic evaluation. Many pieces of body language are an amalgamation of small signs and movements, both voluntary and involuntary. In learning to read body language, therefore, you have to build up from the segments in order to make sense of the whole picture. Jointly and separately, eyebrows, eyes, mouth, skin tone, limbs, fingers, and toes can convey emotions. Think of these bits of body language as the words in a sentence: It makes a lot of sense if you know all the words, but you're only guessing if you have every other word.

To get good at reading body language, go out and do the "R" over and over. Open your eyes and ears. Turn off your biased, over-analytical brain and observe the way a child observes. A toddler sees objects and actions in a more stand-alone way than adults, who go to extraordinary means to make connections. He has no preexisting framework to overlay his observations onto, so he's a much better collector of pure body language than older, well-socialized people. If you place a wrapped box on the table in front of a young child capable of speech, the questions are endless. As you get older, you answer the questions for yourself, assuming you know what everything means.

So as you dive into the following lists, suspend your adult brain. Twist your face into the positions I describe; watch your arms and legs in the mirror as you mimic postures. Watch other people assume these shapes with their face and body—but just to collect information. No judgment is allowed at this stage. Look for similarities, look for differences, and that's it.

It will be easier for you to remove your filters—your blinders—from the E.A.D. parts of the process after you get good at "R." In a way, this is similar to practicing the fundamental moves of a sport before going out to play a game because you want to develop a muscle memory that supports consistent performance.

This top-to-bottom look at body language has two parts:

1. A look at the isolated movements and responses of body.

2. Discussion of how clothes, accessories, body art, and gadgets play a role in your review process. The review is a scan that gives you the puzzle pieces that later will come together in a picture.

This is nothing more than a laundry list to make you aware and open your eyes to some basic concepts. You will never look at yourself or anyone else the same way. I will later address the holistic view, and give you ways to tie it all together so you can read body language.

Super-physical communication

All humans share some communication traits, regardless of culture gender or language. I explore these later in depth, but for now, I want to expose you to essential concepts so the detailed list of body movements in this chapter gets you thinking about how individual gestures might fit into a meaningful, complete picture.

⇒ **Illustrators:** Gestures used to punctuate a statement. Examples are finger pointing; head bobbing; batoning with the hand, arm, or head; and arm outstretched with the palm up, as if to suggest you are giving something.

⇒ **Regulators:** Gestures used to control another person's speech. Examples are putting a hand up like a stop sign; putting a finger to the lips to ask for silence; and moving the hand quickly in a circle as a way of saying, "Speed it up." In the Austin Powers movie, Dr. Evil clamps his fingers over his thumb to suggest his hand is talking whenever he wants his underlings to shut up.

⇒ **Adaptors:** Gestures to release stress, to adjust the body as a way to increase the comfort level. Examples are hand-wringing, neck rubbing, and curling the toes. People often develop idiosyncratic adaptors; they also can look very different depending on whether a man or a woman is doing them. I'll explore these facts later.

⇒ **Barriers:** Postures and gestures we use when we are uncomfortable. Examples include standing behind a table, turning sideways, and, sometimes, crossing arms while in conversation. Everyone has seen someone sitting smugly behind a desk appearing confident and secure. Our primitive ancestors knew the value of such barriering, long before we had desks, and left us a legacy of natural techniques using only the body.

These concepts will help us speak a common language as we spotlight body movements and reactions from scalp to sole.

Forehead

We use our faces, the organ of expression in Desmond Morris's terms, in ways that we rarely realize. Despite the variations, there are some standard expressions associated with the face; by no means are the ones that follow a comprehensive list. However, it does capture fundamental pieces of facial body language.

The billboard you call your forehead allows you to demonstrate the very inner workings of your mind. As a result, the forehead gives residuals. By that I mean it shows what you have been showing. Maybe you've heard the expression "You have the face you deserve by 40." That refers to the contours around the mouth and eyes, particularly, that indicate how much your face has expressed sadness, anger, and other primary emotions in your early years.

I have an astonishing number of lines on my forehead when I wrinkle it and, probably from years of adopting odd facial expressions in interrogations, can use my brow muscles in a way that most people can't. Of course, there may be expressions that other people have mastered that I can't do; the point is that it is possible for an individual to have a unique expression. It also helps that my hair has left for higher ground and instead of a forehead, as the joke goes, I have a fivehead.

Think about what you do with your forehead. Right now, do as many contortions with it that you can, starting with the basics:

⇒ Brows straight up.

⇒ Brows down hard.

⇒ One brow arched.

⇒ Brows knit together in the center.

Look at yourself in the mirror. How many other variations can you manage with those muscles? There is an odd configuration that I can do that involves bringing the brows together while lifting them and jamming the wrinkles in my forehead together. Depending on what I'm doing with my mouth, I either look a deranged killer or a deranged clown.

The brow is one of the most expressive speakers in all non-verbal communication.

Exercise

Put down this book and watch television news, with the sound off, for a few minutes. Take a childlike approach: Look at what's on the screen as if you don't know what to expect. Do you get the sense that these people are telegraphing what is in their head across that well-lit billboard that is the brow?

One movement you will probably notice more than others is the way people use the brow and forehead to emphasize a point or to illustrate what they mean. One type of illustrator is batoning, which is using a body part similar to how a conductor uses a baton. You can shake a hand or finger or your eyebrows or your whole head to drive home your message. Bill O'Reilly often relies on his eyebrows as an illustrator; every day, he gives life to the cliché "brow beating."

Wrinkled forehead

Common reasons to wrinkle the brow include **surprise**, **fear**, or some form of **concern for another**, such as sympathy. The standard ways to express each are:

Surprise is a straight-up lift.

Fear is a lift that engages the muscles between the brows as well. It's the area the French call the "grief muscle," but I prefer to call it the "pain muscle" because you use it both when you express pain and when you want to inflict it.

Surprise   Fear

Someone under very high stress will often massage the pain muscle set between the eyes. This is often involuntary and an adaptor for high stress. I watched a video clip of Lindsey Lohan after her father was arrested. Here is a teenaged star dealing with the scrutiny of millions, raging hormones, accolades from the media that they usually bestow on mature celebrities, and, in the midst of it all, her dad goes to prison. The camera caught her rubbing the area between her eyes so hard that I felt sorry for her. After that, it was no surprise that she manifested more obvious signs of stress, such as losing weight and hard partying.

This is the same gesture that people with tension headaches commonly use. It's an involuntary response to the tightening of the muscles in that area, and an unconscious attempt to stretch them and increase blood flow to the area.

Concern also involves a straight-up lift and use of the pain muscle, but the eyes are engaged very differently. The eyes show sympathy. More on that in the discussion of pupil dilation and contraction.

The absence of a wrinkled brow sends certain messages as well, and two primary ones are calculated deception and Botox injections.

Eyebrows

Brow movement is so integral to human communication that actors get this element of body language right more often than any other part. Does that mean they have talent? Not as much as humanness. I think brow movement is the most inborn trait of human communication. Later in this chapter, I will look closely at one actor who has astonishing brow control: Kevin Spacey.

Eyebrow flash or lift

Eyebrow flash is a fleeting expression with a lifting of the brows as its primary component. This may be instant and disappear quickly. Your eyebrows flash when you **recognize someone**. It's an involuntary and universal response. I've seen it in bringing two prisoners together who assert that they don't know each other. As soon as they see each other, though, the eyebrows go up a little and we know they're lying.

The lack of an eyebrow flash triggers your intuition that someone who should recognize you does not. The next time you see someone you know, pay attention to your brow and his. You expect a mirroring from that person an acknowledgment, even though you aren't conscious of your expectation for that response. When you don't get it, an awkward moment follows. A typical occasion would be your 20-year class reunion. You see someone who used to be the head cheerleader, who looks basically the same as she did in high school. You, on the other hand, have become a marathon runner—a far cry from the pudgy geek who ruled in chemistry class. Your eyebrows flash when she approaches, but she looks straight at you with no sign of ever having seen you before. And she doesn't know body language well enough to fake it.

Compound the eyebrow flash of recognition with a wrinkled brow and here's what you get: I know you, but I'm concerned about where/why/how. One of my body language students told me about being at a party with her husband. They both said "hello" to a man that the husband knew very well professionally, but didn't think she knew. She did know him, though, from parties in years past— before she met her husband. My student described the man's look as an eyebrow flash followed by a knit brow: He clearly recognized them both, but had some concern about seeing them together. She later told her husband the man was probably concerned about what incriminating stories she might pass along.

Your brows also might flash when you **recognize an idea**, as in, "I know what you mean." Similarly, they will jut up as a way of asking the person you're with if she recognizes your idea. It's your body's way of inquiring, "Catch that?"

Eyebrows in "request for approval"

If the eyebrow flash is a snippet of body language, then **request for approval** is its pregnant cousin. Just as in a "catch that" moment, the person is asking whether or not you notice what he is saying. More importantly, with the request for approval he is asking *how* you perceive what he is saying.

When someone is unsure of where he stands, whether he is believed, or how an action is accepted, you will commonly see the eyebrows raise and pause—even if momentarily. The amount of time is an eternity in terms of facial expression. You see it on a regular basis and even do it yourself when you desperately want approval, but until you can identify it as a discrete gesture, you can only do it and respond instinctively, not cognitively. It is the brow version of raising the shoulders into a shrugging motion as a sign of helplessness.

Watch politicians face reporters about touchy issues, or stars field questions about a recent movie. You will see request-for-approval. Kids do it when they attempt something and aren't sure if they got it right, such as tossing a baseball or tying their shoes. Your wife may do it when she comes out of the bedroom with a new dress on. Your husband will do it when he presents you with a box of chocolates for Valentine's Day—a day late. Your new employee will do it when he hands you his first sales report.

When we taped *Torture: The Guantanamo Guidebook* for Channel 4 in the UK, one of the participants was a young Pakistani Brit. *Guidebook* dramatized the types of interrogation procedures that the producers speculated could be going on in U.S. detention centers. The producers had created a scenario in which the Pakistani Brit was a member of a home-grown British terror cell. When I questioned him about why he was in the area he said, "I was just working, not doing anything wrong." Aside from the obvious (who said anything about wrongdoing?), the best indicator was a raising of the brows to exaggerated levels as he spoke. It was a request for approval. Had I allowed it to pass he would have answered the next question feeling as though I approved. Of course I did not. We will address requests for approval in other places as well. The eyebrows are simply the first place we see these requests.

Arching an eyebrow

Some brow movements become associated with cultural norms, such as *Star Trek*'s Mr. Spock raising an eyebrow sharply as he said, "Interesting, Captain." If your mother did a version of this, looking askance at the same time to indicate displeasure, that is her norm, not necessarily a cultural norm. She may, in fact, have picked it up from her mother. Between a mother and child, that expression transmits a specific meaning, whereas the Spock-like raised eyebrow carries a more general message, which is, "Interesting."

Regardless of your mother's meaning, if a person combines this raised brow with a jaundiced eye and a slight smirk, you can bet you have a credibility problem with her.

Lots of people haven't developed the muscle control to arch a single eyebrow, and my experience is that few people can arch both brows separately. One of the few exceptions is our model in this section, Kurtis Kelly. I think it's a matter of practice, but then again, I've observed a correlation between handedness and which eyebrow a person typically raises. Incidentally, Kurtis appears to be ambidextrous in many things.

Try it: raise one eyebrow. Is it your left? Then I'll bet you're right handed.

Brow and eyes in orchestration

You can send a very clear message with a pair of glasses. Raise your brow and look over your glasses. If you're 16, it's funny.

If you're 46, it's **condescending and pushy**. It's an authoritarian look. Looking across the bridge of your nose, even without the glasses, delivers the same effect. If your face is structured correctly, it is a very predatory look; at any rate, the look is one of condemnation.

Take the opposite approach: Tilt your head back and look over your cheekbones without a facial expression at someone. What does this convey? The language is universal, but in English, the description has even become a cliché: looking down your nose at someone. The message of the gesture is so clear that it can effectively be used as a regulator to control conversation.

Absolute brow control

Brows punctuate our messages. If you were capable of absolute brow control, the impact on your communication style would make you surreal. I pride myself on the capacity to become expressionless in interrogations, but this same expressionless face is not useful in conducting interviews and carrying on business and personal relations. Although I believe I can look expressionless, I pale by comparison to Kevin Spacey when it comes to brow control.

As Roger (Verbal) Kint in the brilliant thriller *The Usual Suspects* (1995), Kevin Spacey calmly participates in an interrogation with an obvious *lack* of body language from his brows. Kint refers to himself as a CP (Cerebral Palsy), and exhibits signs of both debilitation and mental impairment, so his oddly still face projects a subhuman quality. (Note: This discussion is necessarily a spoiler, so if you haven't seen the movie, rent it and then come back to this section.) When U.S. Customs agent Dave Kujan (Chazz Palminteri) drops a bombshell, however, Kint shows use of the pain muscle that seems to punctuate genuine surprise at the revelation. (Is the surprise the information itself, or the fact that Kujan has it?)

Later in the movie, when Kujan mentions the name of the noto-rious criminal, Keyser Söze, Kint explodes. Described in various terms as the devil incarnate, Keyser Söze is a powerful force whose very name agitates those who know of him. The logical conclusion from the outburst—one that most law enforcement officers and audience members would draw—is that shock produces involun-tary and universal responses, that is, honest responses. When that happens, many parts of the face reveal the surprise, but particularly the brow. As a corollary, one might conclude that Kint is a dullard who doesn't have the capacity to express feelings normally (hence the lack of brow movement) or he just mimics his prison buddies who stay cool under pressure, but regardless of which scenario is true, ballistic Kint seems like the real deal.

The interrogation proceeds. As Kint seems to develop a sense of comfort, or at least familiarity with Kujan, he begins to tell stories with an animated face. Here is where I got suspicious, because my baseline for him indicated his normal expression was non-expression, so he seemed deceitful when he used his brow in a typically "normal" way. Spacey's Kint soon appears to uncoil, los-ing his control as he talks about the shoot-out, expressing grief over the loss of his friend; there's lot of brow action here. He even makes a disarming statement to Kujan that the reason he didn't run away was that he was afraid—and he accents it perfectly with raised eyebrows, the standard indication of "request for approval."

At the end, we find out just how good an actor Kint is. If there is any screen character who seems to support Desmond Morris's theory about a human being's control over facial muscles, it would be Verbal Kint. We are not dealing with a real human being in Kint, though, we're seeing the output of a gifted actor, Kevin Spacey. He's the mastermind behind the brows that tell nothing and tell everything.

After reviewing other Spacey movies, I now call him the actor with the concrete brow. Control over that usually uncontrollable part of the face is his stock-in-trade, an integral part of his talent. He acts from the brows down until the scene demands a show of emotion, and then he punctuates it with the appropriate brow movement.

Contrast this with the android Data of *Star Trek: The Next Generation*. Poor Data longs to be human, but cannot feel emotion. Eyebrows, corner of the mouth, eyes—everything moves on Data's "emotionless" face. In fact, put him with Captain Picard and Lieutenant Worf, and his face will likely be the most animated.

When John Mark Karr confessed to the killing of JonBenét Ramsey, I watched 45 seconds of the press conference from Thailand in preparation for an interview on Paula Zahn's *Now*. I did not think he was being honest. One of the reasons was a simple flexing of the pain muscle when asked how he got into the house. This should have been a simple question but a quick look of "Oh, sh**! I didn't think of that!" hit his face.

Eyes

A 16th century proverb calls the eyes the windows to the soul. More than 500 years later, the proverb has assumed the stature of gospel. When you really understand the eyes, you'll see how close the proverb is to the mark.

Temples

Moving down the face, we come to areas that surface a lot of involuntary and universal body language: the eyes and areas along the edges of the eyes.

When you do a fake smile, the muscles in the temple area do not move. When you smile up to your eyes—**a real smile**—they crinkle. Only a very small percentage of the population can effect that kind of smile and not mean it.

A baby's smile offers the most genuine vision of happiness on the planet. Nothing is filtered. Nothing is faked.

Pupils

Pupils dilate naturally for several reasons, among them are attraction, fear, and interest. When a human sees **something attractive sexually**, the eyes dilate to get as much of a good thing as possible. Watch the eyes of a heterosexual teenage boy getting his first look at a naked woman.

In the peripheral nervous system, the sympathetic prepares us for fight or flight. The parasympathetic is a breaking mechanism that calms and places us in an un-aroused state. The arousal can be anytime we are in a new situation or a situation perceived as a threat. One of the results of the sympathetic kicking in is that the pupils dilate to take in more data about the threat.

In a normal state of arousal, human pupils are neither dilated nor pinpointed; they are somewhere in between. Pinpointed pupils usually indicate a person does not like what he is looking at, and it can be part of the complex of facial actions that signal rage.

When pupils flash, the sympathetic and parasympathetic are at odds. The sympathetic dilates and the parasympathetic relaxes, so flashing can be continuous or an immediate flash, and then gone. Excitement can cause dilation or pulsing, and so can stress.

Eye movement

Eye movement signals you are **looking for answers inside your head**. The visual cortex is at the back of the brain, so when recalling an image, your eyes will drift upward. The portions of your brain that process sound are located directly over the ears, so when recalling a melody or noise, your eyes will drift toward your ears, usually between the browridge and cheekbone. Cognitive thought and problem solving occur in the frontal lobe in adults. When calculating or analyzing, you will find your eyes—and perhaps your whole head—moving down left. A down-right movement corresponds to intense feelings.

Using questions that target specific sensory channels and specific parts of the brain—visual, auditory, cognitive—you can drive another person to move his eyes. Watch what happens when you pose the following questions to someone:

⇒   What did your first-grade classroom look like?

⇒   What is the 10th word of the "Star Spangled Banner"?

⇒   What is 30 percent of $54?

⇒   What do you think the inside of the Voyager Space Probe looks like?

⇒   What kind of sound does a giraffe make?

⇒   What did you feel when you heard about the deaths of innocents and heroes on 9/11?

This exercise demonstrates that eye movement is natural and linked to brain structures. When someone recalls information from the memory side of the visual cortex, that is visual memory. Visual construct is occurring when the person's eyes move up, but to the side opposite the memory side. Knowing which side is which for an individual helps you develop a baseline. And then you'll know when you ask him a question if he's remembering or creating. You can use the same principle to determine whether someone is remembering a sound or creating one. Finally, except for Basques, who don't seem to fit standard patterns of eye movement, you will see a person who is computing or considering a problem look down left, and someone overcome by emotion looking down right.

While we were working on this book, my co-author attended the final chapel service at a camp near her. Six campers took turns giving short speeches on "what camp means to me." The last speaker, a girl who had just completed her final season at camp, got choked up as she recalled seven seasons of experiences. Maryann noticed that the heads of perhaps a hundred people on the benches in front of her tilted slightly to the right during the emotional speech.

Eyelids

A woman who wears eye makeup ever yday could easily spend $250 a year on her eyelids. Add to that the cost of blepharoplasty, a common procedure to remove excess fat and skin from the eyelids. The American Academy of Facial Plastic and Reconstructive Surgery says 100,000 men and women have it every year; it is possible for a person to spend thousands of dollars in his or her lifetime on those tiny bits of flesh known as eyelids. They must be pretty important.

The makeup and plastic surgery contribute to the passive messages that eyelids convey, primarily, "I'm young(ish). I'm vibrant. I'm sexy." Excess skin around the eyes, even when it occurs in a juvenile, has an aging effect. It makes a person look less awake, and more matronly. People with naturally baggy eyes look tired, or even sad. They don't photograph well, and when they realize that, they may go out of their way to stand behind Grandpa in family photos. Sagging upper lids and puffy lower lids can contribute to some very self-conscious body language, particularly in men and women who spent their youth enjoying the adulation of the opposite sex because of their facial beauty.

An eye twitch signals **stress** unless it's associated with neurological damage. The only way to tell is to observe the person in a completely relaxed state.

An eye droop means the person feels **intense stress**. This is the kind of reaction a prisoner of war might have or person held a gunpoint by a crazed robber. In addition to stress causing a droop in the lower lid, stress engages the sympathetic nervous system, which draws blood from the mucosa and redirects it to the muscles for a fight-or-flight response. The lack of blood causes the lower eyelid to sag in addition to other responses, such as a thinning of the lips.

A much more common sight is that of a child just beginning to understand the concept of object permanence. You see him closing his eyes to make you disappear. Many children, when they first discover this, think that closing his eyes means you can't see him, either. Lids can be used by adults in similar fashion. One way is to close the eyes to prevent seeing something that does not mesh with what they are trying to portray. It helps maintain stability and prevent displaced expectations. Similarly, averting the eyes is not uncommon. We see this in people who do not know how to deal with people with disabilities. The more sophisticated version comes when someone knows you can read eyes, and closes the eyes as a solid barrier against discovery.

In deliberately using eyelids, a person might also do one of the following:

⇒ Close the lids partially as a barrier to further conversation or contact.

⇒ Squeeze one eyelid shut as part of expressing extreme disbelief.

⇒ Wink, as a flirtation, a sign of "okay," or "I understand," or as a request for approval, depending on what the rest of the face is doing.

⇒ Squeeze both eyelids shut to express pain, emotional or physical, or profound concentration.

Blink rate

Everyone has a normal blink rate, which is his baseline. When I ask questions that are not stress-inducing, the rate is constant. When the stress increases, whether from emotional stimulus or fear of discovery that he is lying or bluffing, the blink rate may increase exponentially. I have seen a three to fourfold increase when a person is trying to lie, for example.

Ears

Ears often flush when people are **worried about being discovered**—afraid of being embarrassed, as opposed to already being embarrassed. Some people's ears will blush when they're **bluffing**, too, so watch for that at the poker table.

We might involuntarily send signals by touching our ears, too. As adults, many of us occasionally revert back to the childhood way of blocking out something we don't want to hear by muting the sound. Instead of slamming our palms against our ears and screaming, though, we'll probably rest our head on our hand or brush the ears with fingertips while someone is talking as a symbolic gesture to turn down the volume. People may even do this when they are talking about something that is unpleasant to their own ears, such as a lie. Similar to many adult behaviors, this is an echo of something that has worked in our past.

Pulling the ear or lightly rubbing the ear are both common gestures, but they don't send any particular message by themselves—unless you're Carol Burnett. She used to tug on her ear at the end of each show to let her grandmother know she was okay. Rubbing or pulling an ear could be just gestural **space-fillers** for a person, indicating "I'm thinking" or "I'm bored." You'll need other indicators to conclude that this means that the person is nervous, for example, flushed ears or eyes reaching hard to the construct side of the brain while the action occurs.

For some people, ears are an erogenous zone, so you should look at how the person touches her ear. Is it a delicate touch? Rough rubbing? A little scratch? Self-stroking the ear is one of many adapters that involve touching the skin to provide comfort.

Nose

Knowing as much as I think I do about physiology, I was still amazed at how many vessels are in the nose while at a recent exhibit featuring human bodies. The exhibit relies on a technique called plastination, which sucks moisture from cadavers and then coats and fills them with plastic. This preserves the bodies and allows them to be placed into static positions so that viewers can examine musculature, nerves, the circulatory system, and so on. It allows for a unique view of organs and other body parts that have been sliced like onions. The nose on display consisted of so many plastic-filled blood vessels that it appeared to be one solid mass. This showed vividly how many blood vessels populate the nose. It's the most sensitive part of the body, due in large part to its vascularity.

A person **under stress** will commonly touch her nose, whether it's a light scratch or a rub. Just touching the nose doesn't signal stress, however. Sometimes touching the nose means a person is **disgusted** with something. The whole gesture will be different from a stress gesture, however. It could be a wipe with the back of a hand (when there's no reason to wipe), or a finger joint laid against the nose, as if to block something stinky from making its way inside.

As opposed to what many people think—and one indicator of this is how many journalists have asked me to affirm this in interviews—you cannot tell whether or not a person is lying just because he's scratching his nose. You can tell that if he's doing excessive nose handling that something is going on in his head, however, because he's probably responding to increased vascular action.

Wrinkling the nose in **disgust** is almost always a female gesture. Many men cannot seem to do it.

Mouth

In glancing through *Time* magazine's fall 2006 supplement on "The Art of the Luxury Deal" (not my usual reading), I noticed page after page of models with their mouths slightly open. It's probably an attempt to project sexy and vulnerable, but this mouth position is often part of the "stupid look"—the look of mouth breathers.

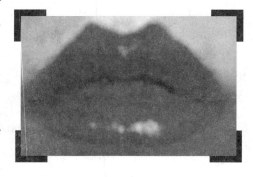

When the model combines it with a blank stare, she looks brain dead. So, if the object is to get across that she's no threat, the photographer certainly succeeded. Note: None of the male models had this look.

When done in combination with a wrinkled brow, pulling the corners of the mouth down signals **disgust**.

Take this same pulled-down mouth and add the raised brow of recognition and you have a very different message: "I did not know that, but I do understand it."

Covering the mouth is a simple barrier loaded with meaning. It could mean so many things that this gesture provides a great example of the importance of context. Why would anyone cover his or her mouth?

⇛   Trying to eat and talk at the same time, which is a gesture hugely affected by culture.

⇛   Self-conscious about her teeth.

⇛   Shy; unwilling to smile broadly because it is uncomfortable.

⇛   Doesn't want you to hear what she's saying and this is a barrier thrown up subconsciously to mute the sound.

Although I explore combinations of moves later, I'll start moving into the topic here. If a person is self-conscious about her teeth, she'll first signal that by drawing her lips down over her teeth, smiling with lips together. Notice that this close-lipped smile may even engage the muscles at the corner of her eyes. That means it's a genuine smile, and just because she doesn't show teeth is not an indication of any bad feelings or deceit. That smile can offer just as much, or more, warmth as the toothiest grin.

When a person's **mind is completely engaged**, he may unconsciously do things with his mouth that are odd, and almost abusive. Chewing on the inside of the mouth, licking the lips repeatedly, sticking the tongue out, biting a lip, or biting chapped skin on the lip (maybe even causing bleeding), and twisting the mouth to the side are among common movements. What his eyes are doing give away more of the story. Look for signs of emotion (down right), calculation (down left), and so on.

Another completely involuntary move that a mouth will make is the quiver resulting from being startled. I saw a clerk drop an armful of hangers in a store recently and that's what her mouth did. She said nothing, but the shaking lower lip and chin displayed surprise. So much communication in one second with no words—and there was no way she could have controlled what happened to her because the movement was a purely stimulus-response gesture. Would any human respond the same way? No, and the reasons are varied. Someone less sensitive to noise might not have reacted that way. Someone who didn't care about dropping hangers in front of store customers might not have reacted that way. Someone who dropped the hangers because she was distracted by another occurrence in the store might not have responded that way, either.

Lips

Another movement that also involves the mouth is licking the lips. Children lick their lips when they're thinking, as do horses, as well as a lot of adults. It's one sign that the **brain is engaged**. Lip biting can also signal thinking, but suggests a more stressful topic, as I mentioned previously.

Men will sometimes purse and grip their lips so their lips almost disappear. Often, that is a man **holding back emotion**. In the video of Lyndon Johnson at the Democratic National Convention that chose John F. Kennedy over him to be the presidential candidate, he leaks frustration, annoyance, and even anger when

he's faced with the "opportunity" to be vice president. His lips assume a sucked-in grimace, and he tilts his head down during speaking. Even though the words coming out of his mouth are conciliatory "...my friend, John F. Kennedy...," his body language says that he was choking back emotion.

Fight or flight has an impact on the lips as well. When the sympathetic kicks in it gives blood to things needed for fight or flight: muscles, lungs, and heart. It takes blood away from "useless" things such as the highly evolved primate brain and the reproductive and the digestive systems. A direct result is blood leaving all mucosa. This means the lips become drawn and thin.

Unlike fight-or-flight demands, the mucous membranes need more blood flow in times of sexual arousal. Because the body requires high blood flow for erections, sensitivity, and lubrication, the body floods mucosa with blood. The result is red cheeks and full lips. We can see it in both men and women. It is the reason that the Angelina Jolie "pillow lip" has become so admired. It is a sure sign of attraction in a woman, and easy for even the least perceptive of men to recognize as a come-on look.

Smile

Another facial sign, but one that varies from person to person, is the smile. Here is the difference between a practiced, perfect C-shaped smile and a smile that rises to the eyes: one is for presentation, and one is genuine.

My natural, genuine smile is a little crooked. A sort of half-smile. But when I'm meeting someone for the first time or smiling for the television cameras, I will give a balanced smile. Take a look at people you know well and notice the difference between their relaxed smile and the one they use as part of establishing control.

Happy smile   Business smile

As I mentioned, a smile that doesn't reach the eyes broadcasts insincerity; the person doesn't look happy even if a grin is present.

I've often contemplated the origins of a human smile because I've watched so many animals bare their teeth in what might be described as a smile. In a chimp, a smile means fear. Did our human smiles develop as a way of making ourselves less threatening to other chimps? Perhaps our ancestors found the smile a quick way of alerting another chimp that they had no intention of causing harm. They chose to express fear so they would not be perceived as a threat. Both chimps would put their guard down and everyone remained alive.

When baby horses walk up to adult horses, for about the first year of their lives they will do something that we might call a smile.

Once again, however, it's the fear expression that communicates to adults, "I'm weaker than you. Don't hurt me."

A few of the common smiles that communicate a distinct message are these:

⇒ When President George W. Bush says something and wants to know whether or not his audience will approve of it, he makes a goofy, country-boy smile. You can tell when he's uncertain about how people will perceive him.

⇒ Movie stars on the red carpet often use a camera smile. It's even, teeth showing, and no engagement of the muscles around the eyes. This is a polite, public smile.

⇒ The amused smile is one you see among audience members at the Oprah Winfrey show when someone on stage says something mildly humorous. It engages the temple muscles, but exposure of teeth is limited or nonexistent.

⇒ For an example of the seductive smile, think Sharon Stone in *Basic Instinct*.

⇒ A smile of recognition shows genuine happiness if you like the person, and simple politeness if you do not. Regardless of the form it takes, it always involves the involuntary eyebrow flash associated with recognizing someone.

⇒ A smile of discomfort often appears on the face of the spouse being dragged to a 20th high school class reunion, or on the face of a shy 13-year-old boy who's meeting the new, pretty girl at school.

Jaw

A stern jaw typically conveys anger, as opposed to a slack jaw, which sends a message, "I am non-threatening—and I'm stupid."

My slight overbite gives me a naturally angry, domineering look. I can look a lot harsher with an overbite than someone who has an underbite. It's hard to look stern when you don't have a chin. The jaw is a powerful symbol. My interrogator buddies and I have speculated that maybe only men with a big, square jaw and overbite ought to be in the business. Combine the male set jaw with brows drawn together in anger and my beady eyes, and you have the picture of someone who looks intimidating. It's the core segment of a body-language picture designed to instill fear.

Consider how different this jaw is on a woman's face. It can be comical, as comedians such as Carol Burnett and her Tarzan howling, and Debra Messing and her bulldog scowling have shown. Men, too, have taken advantage of the comic possibilities of the large jaw and the fact that it enables the kind of rubbery facial expressions of Jim Carrey.

Contrast the big-mouthed, full-jawed look of some women such as Julia Roberts with the tiny mouthed picture of Bernadette Peters. Julia Roberts can play the range of emotions from silly to sorrowful to nasty, partly because her facial structure supports that range. Can Bernadette Peters ever look fierce? She can sound vicious, but that little mouth of hers opens and I still see cute—despite the fact that her talent is expansive.

Given that she is talented, let's envision her as a heinous criminal. Combine that angelic mouth with an expressionless brow as she tells you how she is going to kill you. The result is surreal and disturbing because it doesn't fit any of our preconceived notions.

Head and neck

Head tilts often **correspond with the eye movement** previously described. For example, the down-right look of someone in a state of deep emotion may also involve the entire head plunging down right, which is a posture you will see at funerals. Head tilts or bobs may also serve to **reinforce a statement or substitute for it**. The sharply cocked head indicating, "You don't really mean that" needs no words behind it. And a head moving similar to a bobble-head doll, at least in the American culture, suggests uncertainty. In watching disgraced Tour de France cyclist Floyd Landis and his wife on the *Today* show, I saw Amber Landis move her head back and forth like that when Matt Lauer asked her if she believed her husband's claim of innocence. Her voice said, "Yes," but her head said, "I don't know." I had already determined that Landis's body language leaked deceit; his wife's action reinforced my analysis.

Another type of head tilt is the raised chin, typically done deliberately to express **indignation**. Take notice how often this occurs in interview/talk shows. When I analyzed a tape for *US Weekly* of Larry King interviewing Jennifer Aniston, I noticed she raised her chin when he asked a personal question that she did not, and would not, answer. It was an honest, involuntary way of gesturing, "I don't have to answer that."

The neck has throbbing veins and arteries that can indicate temporary stress or a chronic condition such as hypertension. Rubbing the neck is an instinctive reaction to discomfort that can be associated with distended veins, or just a sense that neck is warm and a cool hand on it would feel good. Every touch does not convey information about someone's emotional state. Sometimes an itch is just an itch.

Limbs

Shoulders

One surprising result from my TV watching related to this book was observing Michael Dorn's movements as the Klingon Worf in *Star Trek: The Next Generation*. I laughed as I watched him display anger with rounded shoulders, a jaw that was tucked down, and open hands. Lieutenant Worf, I have news for you: this is the body language of an angry woman.

Shoulders back on a man or woman conveys **control and alertness**, which is why everyone in the U.S. military either stands that way when called to attention or faces the prospect of a weekend learning how to do it right.

And unlike Worf, men will throw their shoulders back and flare their upper back muscles (if they know how), as a sign of **power**, with or without anger.

Arms

In the discussion of categories of gestures that follows this section, you will see how much we use our arms as a means to punctuate points made verbally, as well as to let other people know what they should or should not be doing. We flail, point elbows, and use them similar to how a conductor uses a baton. We move them forward to shut people out and open them to let people in. Most of the combination gestures I will explore later will involve face and arms.

In any analysis of the meaning of limb movement, the first three things to consider are height, culture, and build. In baselining someone to read body language, these must be part of the picture or your conclusions could be way off.

An older gentleman at the resort where I was staying recently caught my eye as he gestured to the other people at his dinner table. I couldn't hear anything he said, but I concluded from the way he raised his hands in the air that he was not American, British, or Germanic. He looked as though he could be Italian, but he wasn't close enough for me to be sure. To satisfy my curiosity, I maneuvered closer to him the next day when I saw him near the pool. From listening to the conversation, I understand that he was from Argentina.

⇒   Man who gestures with hands low: British, Germanic

⇒   Man who gestures with hands high: Mediterranean, Latin

Mediterranean and Latin people have a full-bodied approach to conversation, with the hands moving at face level. Germanic people have a natural tendency to gesticulate with the hands below shoulder level, although media trainers sometimes succeed in getting their executive and politician clients to gesticulate higher for the cameras. When I was doing a lot of theater and studying to portray an old man, I wondered, "What makes an old man look old?" One thing I soon realized is that old Anglo men don't raise their elbows above their waist.

Examine the differences between effeminate gay and straight. Why does Jack McFarland in *Will & Grace* look so much more flamboyant than Will Truman, who is also gay? Watch how he moves his arms—how high they are—as compared to Will the lawyer, who has less flagrant displays of passion. Will looks more stereotypically masculine, even doing the same family of gestures, because his movements are lower.

Hips

If a man puts his hands on his hips, it means **defiance**, as long as his fingers are pointed toward his crotch. It's an obvious symbol of masculinity.

Women typically put their hands on their hips with fingers pointed toward the butt cheeks

to show the same emotion. If a man does that, some may perceive it as looking stereotypically gay.

Contrast a man and a women standing arrogantly and cocky. One demonstrates masculinity by framing the genitals and the other demonstrates feminine power by pointing toward her assets in the rear. Displays of power make us exaggerate the gestures of the gender with which we identify.

Legs

I'm tall with relatively thick legs, so I generally sit either with my legs in a "V" or with one foot slung over the opposite leg. A few years ago, I was doing an interview with *Der Spiegel* with my legs in the latter position and the reporter accused me of being cocky. "That's not cocky, that's relaxed," I explained to her. My build doesn't allow me to sit comfortably with my legs crossed similar to a "European gentleman."

A woman can make a deliberate **power statement** by sitting with her legs crossed and her high heel pointed at someone. It is a statement about confidence through sexuality, confidence through taste in selecting that shoe, and assertiveness by aiming the heel at the person. The message: *Yes, I'm a woman, but I can deal with you like a man; I have power here.* It is an attempt to emasculate.

Legs can move back and forth as a result of nervous energy. I have often seen young men sitting with the legs moving back and forth. This is a comforting move as the thighs and genitalia make contact. Few, if any, realize they are doing it.

Extremities

Hands

Most of what I'll tell you about hands will be in the section on holistic expressions because a majority of meaningful hand gestures involve other body parts. The fig-leaf posture is one example (at right). Watch men of different cultures in diverse situations do it. The one thing they have in common if they feel the least bit threatened is an involuntary compulsion to, in a phrase that J.R.R. Tolkein's Golem would use, "protect the precious."

Fidgeting hands, picking at cuticles, and an autoerogenous finger rubbing are all potentially signs of stress and/or attempts at stress relief. But again, without context, what you may be observing is nothing more than an annoying personal habit.

Grooming of the hands sends messages, too, but they may be mixed. In interrogation, I might ask a source, "What do you do?"

He replies, "I'm a clerk," but I notice that he has callused hands. Should I believe him? When I meet someone who asks what I do, I might say, "Consultant, author, speaker." But my hands are callused, bruised, and it wouldn't be uncommon for a broken bone to show. Should you believe me? The meaning in both cases is that, either the person is lying, or he does something in his spare time that tears up his hands. I have my horses and Medieval battle re-creations to blame, but a source in the battlefield could tell a story to explain his calluses that may or may not be true. Good questioning gets the story behind the body language, and it can give you an edge in both business and personal relationships.

Grooming practices with hands become almost unconscious because people tend to look at their hands more than other body parts. I have a theory about this: Hands are the only tools we own from birth. There may be no significant meaning at all associated with pushing back the cuticles during a meeting, for example. If it is a sign of anything, it probably means the person is a little bored rather than stressed. If a person without well-groomed hands tries to cover them up in your presence, that's a sign she's **embarrassed**, or at the very least, **feels insecure** around you. Curling hands is a similar sign.

When you see someone do something bizarre with his hands, he may raise questions in your mind. If someone repeats a gesture over and over, such as a secret signal that designates a member of the notorious gang MS-13, for example, it stays with you in some form. The Army had a number of unofficial hand signals, too, such as this one:

In Army parlance, it meant, "Cover me, I'm f*c*ed," or in polite terms, "My weapon's jammed." One former Army guy may sneak it to another former Army guy in a business meeting and no one would know about his cry for help.

Feet

A person can have many reasons for crossing his feet; you definitely need context to know whether or not that means he is shutting you out. Take his anatomy into account for starters. A tall person in a low chair will either have his feet crossed or his knees in his ears. A woman who was raised to adopt "modest" posture will habitually cross her feet because her mother spent 18 years telling her that's how ladies sit.

Contrast with that the subconscious act of turning the toes inward, an action that reflects **subjugation**, especially in a sexual situation. Young women will often sit with their toes turned inward in sexual circumstances where they are not in charge. Something deep inside her "orders " her to adopt a submissive pose.

People in **stressful situations** will commonly point their feet toward the door. In interviewing management candidates for Trane, this is one thing I've noticed many times. When I'm teaching, I have people sit on a table for certain body language demonstrations. I enjoy having the class observe the crossed feet, flexed feet, and feet pointed toward the door as I jack up the anxiety level.

The grooming of the feet is usually less obvious than the hands, of course, but in sandal weather or intimate situations where someone's bare feet are exposed to you, grooming can say a lot about issues of femininity, athleticism, and basic hygiene. Showing ugly feet in sandals may be comfortable, but you can expect some people to think less of you. And then there's the extreme: I saw a man with ugly feet walking barefoot through a Wal-Mart outside of Atlanta, Georgia. When I see someone walking around barefoot in public, I think of that as an absolute disdain for cultural norms.

Utterances

In addition to proximity, time, movement, culture, and other essential topics in the field of body language, an important area of study is vocalics. I call it "utterances," and I refer to vocal, but not verbal, communication. *Ah, hmmm, ick, ewww, yuck,* and *uh* are a few of them and roles they play in communication can vary:

⇒ They change the pace of communication.

⇒ They fill otherwise dead air, but don't necessarily tell you much. Watch eye movement, hands, tilt of the head, and so on to find out if the utterance is an expression of visualizing, disgust, confusion, creation, and so on.

⇒ Depending on what vocal quality you pick up— strident, lyrical, coarse, breathy—you will get a sense of the person's emotions.

In reviewing body language, you will also pick up utterances that relate to tone or pronunciations that seem abnormal to you. These can be subtle aspects of speech that give away information about a person's port of origin. I don't mean a full-blown Boston accent or my Georgia-boy style of talking, I'm referring to the way many Northern Americans and Canadians pronounce "ou," and the way people from Pennsylvania Dutch country have a tendency to go up in pitch at the end of a sentence and down when asking a question. If you pick that up, you have an extra clue about sub-cultural influences: If the person lived in that area, or with people from that area long enough to pick up such a regionalism, then chances are good that the body language shows it, too.

The impact of disability

With disability comes an adaptation of human behavior in the same sense as adapting to a new culture. Communication may take on forms not considered typical by the society. Looking at it from the outside, the result may place the disabled person in a sub-typical role. Looking at it from the inside, the result may be that the disabled person wants to prove how typical or super-typical she is.

If a birth defect places the person in a life-long struggle to overcome the sub-typical role, imagine the struggle when the disability occurs in adult life through trauma or disease. Franklin Delano Roosevelt was 39 years old when polio struck and paralyzed both of his legs up to the hips. Imagine the impact. FDR fought for normalcy through rehabilitation that was both costly and difficult. How did this impact his sense of belonging and later even his polices of entitlement of average Americans?

Regardless of the type of disability, physically challenged people have something in common: steps, curbs, and banks of snow present problems. Similar to a red-headed woman I once met who thought we should stick together because of our hair color, some people find unity in physical adversity; others live their lives as if it's irrelevant. As we look more closely at the holistic view of body language in Chapter 5, you will see how this manifests itself in open *versus* closed movements—even in cases when disability severely limits movement.

Disability can blind people on the outside to the real person and how the person's culture impacts her psyche. The natural reaction of an unaffected person is to feel guilt and remorse and to over-accommodate, which is in its own style treating the person as sub-typical. Activists such as Marta Russell criticized Mother Teresa for building a homeless shelter in New York City without elevators to accommodate the disabled. She responded that an elevator is a luxury that would cost soup and sandwiches. I'll extrapolate to say that Mother Teresa concluded that the needs of a great number of sub-typical people—the homeless in New York—surpassed the needs of a minority, who may not be sub-typical at all. (And are we to think that the good sisters wouldn't walk downstairs to give a sandwich to a homeless man in a wheelchair?)

Body adornments

Body language encompasses both voluntary and involuntary movements, but you should not stop there. In some cases, hair, clothing, accessories, and body art can clarify the message, or are even an integral part of it. In others, they distract from the meaning. *Sex and the City*'s Carrie Bradshaw droops without her Manolo Blahniks. Her shoes enable her body language; they affect the way she expresses resilience and optimism. You can't know Carrie without knowing her shoes. Contrast this with the case of the Toronto police officer who got away with murder for 30 years. Finally convicted in 1999 with the help of DNA evidence, Ron West had shot and killed two women with young children at home. They saw him at the door and let him in. Any suspicion they might have gleaned from his body language no doubt faded because his police uniform projected trust and protection.

Most people consciously choose their appearance. It may relate to lifestyle and occupation, but within the limits of those, we usually still have some range about hairstyles, clothes, and body art. They are an outcrop of how we want people to perceive us, and how we fit in our culture.

Many people exercise control over those elements with a great deal of intent and awareness of their "audiences," but some people unintentionally send the wrong message. In reading body language, therefore, you have to analyze intent as well as outcome. For example, soldiers, strippers, and ex-cons used to be the only people I knew who had tattoos. Now, tattoos are part of the body language of youth. It is tribalism: the ability to go to a new place and adapt to a new person because you are recognized as part of a group. Unfortunately, some people still think that only soldiers, strippers, and ex-cons have tattoos, and they project that in conversation with anyone who has a tattoo. Not long ago, a couple of my Army students blurted out "tramp stamp" when they saw a young woman's lower-back tattoo. In a rather heated conversation with the offenders, she made it clear that it was nothing more than body art complimenting her fashionable, hip-hugging jeans.

In learning to R.E.A.D., therefore, you will learn the relative importance of what is on the body as well as what it does. As I did with body parts, I'll start with the scalp and quickly work down to the toes in looking at body adornments.

Hairstyles offer great insights into intent. The woman who gives me a flat top told me that people come in often and ask for a hairstyle that is impossible to deliver. They want a Mohawk even though they have a receding hairline and bald spots, or they want long, bouncy curls made out of fine, thin hair. They get mad at her when she can't deliver because they believe that if they want a particular style, she should be able to create it. They want to send a message; they insist on it, whether or not it makes sense.

Long hair on a man who is mostly bald looks very odd to me, but for those men who choose that style, it expresses their freedom. I make an assumption that they will be forthcoming about their point of view in a conversation, rather than bend to cultural norms about restraint. A 40ish woman who lets her hair go completely gray projects the message, "I haven't tampered with myself." Emmy Lou Harris is a great example of someone in that category.

Hats can have a simple, utilitarian function or project a definite message. What conclusions do you draw when you see a cowboy hat on someone who's not a cowboy, a baseball hat on backwards, or a hat that goes perfectly with an outfit?

Many people have told me I look good in a cowboy hat. I only wear it when I'm riding, however, because I'm not comfortable strutting through downtown Atlanta looking like I should be yelling, "Yee haw" at the hot dog vendor.

This comfort factor—having the outside match the image of oneself on the inside—is why a woman might develop a "relationship" with a designer, whether she's investing in haute couture or buying off the rack. She feels that the designer understands her personality as well as functional requirements related to the garment. Oleg Cassini designed more than 300 outfits as the personal couturier for Jacqueline Kennedy during her days as First Lady. His clothes framed her charisma. Even a young woman with less money than a Kennedy will clearly reveal something about her personality by choosing Ralph Lauren over Laura Ashley.

Part of this experience is tribal, too. It is human nature to want to express identity through a "look" and to enhance a sense of belonging through dress.

I know a woman who is, as we say in the South, "too poor to paint, too proud to whitewash." (For Northern readers, that phrase is applied to old-money Southerners who do not have any old or new money, but they still have the house. They don't want anyone to know they don't have any money, though, so they let the fence rot rather than spruce it up with lime and water.) This woman tries to identify herself through a "classic" look, even though she would look a lot more presentable if put the put the moth-eaten "classics" back in the steamer trunk and spent $100 at Wal-Mart. But to her, "new" equals "bad."

Watches and pens are extensions of body language, too. If you have an expensive watch, and you aren't on the *Forbes* 100 list, you might use gestures and wear shirts and jackets that allow you show off that $10,000 timepiece.

You can tell if someone is stuck in a period through things similar to this as well. A perfect example: Flower children wearing organic cotton skirts still live in Berkeley, California, although instead of being 20-something babes, they're now 60-something grandmothers.

Finally, why "every shoe tells a story" is not only a question to be answered here, it is one tackled in *National Geographic* by senior writer Cathy Newman. She quotes both designers and historians in unequivocally pointing to the effect of shoes on body language, the statements that shoes make about social status, and the roles shoes play in projecting intent. (Cathy Newman, *National Geographic,* September 2006, pp. 74–93). Among the most salient points are:

⇒ The blatant sexual body language that very high heels force: breasts out, butt out, and the perception of a longer leg.

⇒ Conveying wealth by having the soles of a shoe—or in the case of the Sioux, a moccasin—dirt-free. The Sioux used their clean, beaded moccasins as sign that they could afford to ride horses rather than walk.

⇒ Expressing an attitude. Newman describes some of the made-to-order shoes in Olga Berluti's Warrior collection, priced at $4,000 to $12,000 a pair, as "shoes with the sleek, managing profile of a mako shark, shoes decorated with piercings, tattoos, sometimes scars…shoes for the hidden warrior inside every man."

⇒ Allowing the style to have a transformative effect. This is the story of the woman who wears sensible heels to office, and then comes home and replaces them with stiletto-heeled, thigh-high boots.

You don't even have to polish the soles of your shoes, as former *Vogue* editor Diana Vreeland reportedly did, to be "well-heeled," which is a phrase that really means something in our culture. Someone with worn, unpolished shoes translates into "poor," or at least "careless," throughout the country.

As a former soldier, "well-heeled" takes on another meaning for me. Anyone who spends hours every day running and hiking in boots understands that they are the most important part of your outfit. Your feet are everything.

Contrast that with the argument that sacrificing comfort for style can be so psychologically rewarding that the mental pain of wearing "good " shoes (that is, good for foot health) is devastating. The psychological comfort is more important than the physical comfort. A pointy-toed Manolo Blahnik may indeed, as Newman says, be a "corset for the foot," but I'm told that a woman who wears it can experience a kind of euphoria. She quotes Madonna as saying that Manolo Blahniks are as good as sex and "last longer."

Shoes can also become the symbol of one's core identity. You've met the person who is a runner and wears sneakers all the time, everywhere—from the garden to church. Running is her life and the sneakers are her anchor. They say, "This is not only what I do, it's what I am."

And now for the man's perspective: A word about cowboy boots is in order. I've worn cowboy boots—really good ones—and sneakers, and sneakers are more comfortable. I wear boots in an airport, even though I know I will have to go through the exercise of taking them off for security and then putting them back on. What does that say about my willingness to sacrifice comfort for style?

My point is that, if you are uncomfortable in your clothes, you will be demonstrably less confident. Your body language will bleed that discomfort.

Don't project too much in analyzing body adornments, though. You can read something into accessories, clothes, or body language that is yours, not his. For example, I usually clip my cell phone to my jeans pocket. It looks very cowboyish, reminiscent of the gun in a holster, I'm told. The reason I hook it there is because my belt—my favorite belt that I wear almost every day—costs a lot more than my jeans and I don't want to scratch it. Sometimes a cigar is just a cigar.

Move toward the holistic

"Review" is its own, complete exercise. Look at people around you and catalogue similarities and differences. Gather your own pictures of people, and then review them as you become more and more conscious of your filters and how they affect your judgments of body language. You need to move to a point at which you can look clinically at people.

What you don't want to do is create Frankenstein's monster in using body language—piecing together hands, eyes, feet, and words to create an incongruous picture.

Gesturing, With or Without Intent

Continue to keep your mind on "review" in this short chapter. You will still be looking at isolated movements, but from a different angle. In some cases, I'll take you behind the gesture to examine intent, and in others, I'll take you behind the gesture to see why it "just happens," that is, there is no intent.

This activity is still part of what interrogators call "passive observation," which means watching the source to collect a range of useful information. "Active observation" follows it and involves asking questions of people around the source, similar to fellow prisoners and prison guards. It isn't until after those stages are complete that we move beyond observation and into evaluation, analysis, and decisions—the E.A.D. in R.E.A.D. Everything related to "R" is an external process and everything related to E.A.D. reflects internal processes.

In teaching body language, I categorize gestures that carry standard meanings into several categories: symbols, illustrators, regulators, adaptors, and barriers. I also associate mirroring with this group because it is a standard technique, which can be involuntary or intentional, for forging a bond with someone. Symbols and mirroring have their roots in culture, whereas the others are more universal expressions. I'm going to put rituals in this discussion as well, because they are gestures people repeat (they may be standard for an entire culture or they may be standard for a single individual) that may have enormous meaning, or they may have no meaning whatsoever.

Symbols

Symbols such as a kiss, sticking out your tongue, and waving hello capture particular sentiments. Gestures similar to these are learned expression of thought and can vary sharply from culture to culture. In every case, though, they represent a whole thought and convey a standard meaning as long as you replicate the context for them. For example, if you ask me a question to which the answer is yes, you will always understand that my nodding means yes, if the context is correct:

⇒   I understand your language.

⇒   I am American and nodding means "yes" in my country.

⇒   The up-and-down movements in the nod are done in relatively quick succession.

Although a symbol is very cultural, as the culture spreads, it can become super-cultural. A good example is "thumbs up," which international peace-keeping troops with no single, common language could use with each other. Contrast that with the sign of fingers raised in a "V." To Americans who served in World War II, they see "Victory." To Baby Boomers, it's a peace sign. To a lot of Brits, it is a way of flipping someone off if done with the back of the hand toward the person. The supposed root of this is that warriors would display their V-shaped fingers to the dying enemy they had just hit with an arrow. The two fingers they held up had released the deadly shaft.

Symbolic gestures can become a rich unspoken language when the gestures carry a clear and succinct meaning, as is the case in military hand signals, such as the "cover me" example in the last chapter. The driving point is, through some cultural change, all communicating parties learn the accepted meaning.

Illustrators and regulators

Illustrators and regulators are punctuation. Their power may be learned by watching mom or dad, or people on TV—that is, culture influences the shape of them—but they are still gestures that come "naturally." Examples of illustrators are finger pointing as you accuse a person of something and using your forearm to drive home your point. Regulators include using your hand similar to a stop sign or dragging your extended fingers across your throat to say "Cut."

One of the classic signs of punctuating a message is batoning. President Bill Clinton used this illustrator in his public rebuttal of the accusation that he'd had an affair with Monica Lewinsky. His batoning forearm and hand emphasized every word of his denial. Adolph Hitler did it as part of his wild gesticulation that whipped his audience into submission. Television evangelists do it to hammer on each and every word in a key Bible passage.

Although gesturing with symbols must be learned, illustrators do not have to be learned. Any movement can become an illustrator if used to drive home the message. Watch as a sassy teenager throws a shirt on the counter and huffs out of the store. Even if she never says, "I don't have time to wait for a dressing room!" her action illustrates her thoughts. Even a gesture such as flashing the middle finger can become an illustrator when used to punctuate thoughts.

Other examples of illustrators are:

⇛ Finger pointing, either as an accusation or designation.

⇛ Use of any body part to baton. A head tilt, finger wag, foot shake, or movement of the entire upper body could be an illustrator.

⇛ Opening the lips to overly enunciate each word.

⇛ Closing the lids and tilting the head as you slowly speak to someone who just doesn't get it.

⇛ Placing the palms together in a prayerful motion as you plead your case.

⇛ Placing the fingers to the lips while thinking.

Bill O'Reilly uses regulators all the time, as do most of the news talk hosts who invite argument. When he's had his fill of a guest's comments, the hand goes up and he may slightly tilt his head, barrier with the eyelids, and jump in with his viewpoint. If he can't shut him up that way, he may combine both hands with a facial gesture that says "Enough": raised eyebrows, pursed lips, and set jaw.

Regulators do not need to be elaborate or well understood. Simply questioning someone's veracity has the effect of slowing or halting a line of conversation.

⇒   A "talk to the hand motion."

⇒   A shocked gasp.

⇒   A roll of the eyes.

⇒   Placing the hands to pain muscle between the eyes.

⇒   Looking up while exhaling.

Other simple and common versions of the regulator include:

⇒   Pointing to someone as if to say, "Your turn."

⇒   Placing your hand on someone.

⇒   Tilting the head to indicate interest (a very female regulator).

⇒   Simply nodding as someone speaks to encourage that behavior.

⇒   Shaking the head to discourage behavior.

Adaptors

Adaptors are a way that the body tries to comfort itself. The primary cause of this is discomfort due to a real or perceived threat, or boredom. The body will invent innumerable ways to do this, but in true human fashion, we have developed standard ways as well. Because adaptors are often gender-specific, I will go into greater detail about them in the discussion of filters. The key thing to know at this stage is that reflect energy displacement is a way to relieve stress.

Why does a baseball player rub his legs before grabbing the bat?

(a) Wipe the sweat off his hands.

(b) Wipe the dirt off his hands.

(c) Relieve stress.

He has gloves and pine tar on his hands, so he isn't doing (a) or (b). The gesture is an adaptor.

Other examples of adaptors are:

⇒ Fidgeting of nearly any kind.

⇒ Rubbing fingertips together.

⇒ Wobbling legs back and forth while seated (a typically male adaptor).

⇒ Tapping.

⇒ Scratching.

⇒ Grooming.

⇒ Picking.

⇒ Rubbing a body part.

Barriers

Barriers show you are uncomfortable with a threat. People find scores of ways to block out the offender. Here are some examples, although I want to point out that doing one of these things doesn't necessarily make it a barrier. Context is all-important.

⇒ Standing behind a table.

⇒ Crossing your arms.

⇒ Turning sideways while in conversation.

⇒ Putting your purse or briefcase between you and other person.

⇒ Lowering your eyelids during conversation.

⇒ Putting your arm on a table between you and the person next to you.

⇒ Holding up reading materials.

As I noted in Chapter 3, a common protective gesture men use is to barrier the genitals by crossing their hands. Watch men on TV game shows who are unaccustomed to making public appearances. Even though some of them are behind a podium, you will see their hands down in a fig-leaf position—that's a double barrier. It's a natural movement for men to cover their genitals when they are under any kind of stress.

One of the news stories of 2005 involved a monkey who attacked a California man who had brought a birthday cake to the animal sanctuary for another monkey. Feeling threatened—

the birthday monkey had earned 39 candles, so it must have been a blazing cake—the attacking monkey did what came naturally: he ripped the testicles off his adversary. Alpha-males do things similar to this, which is why "protecting the precious" is a posture ingrained in men. No thought is involved; it's pure instinct.

Driving through the outskirts of a small town last summer, I encountered a line of three cars that had been stopped by a woman on the road crew. She and her counterpart about two-tenths of a mile down the road relayed the status to each other; one would flash her "slow" sign while the other flashed her "stop" sign so that one lane of traffic could move through at all times. For some reason, my side continued to stare at a "stop" sign for more than a minute—too much for the drivers in front of me. They did U-turns.

It was too much for the stop-sign holder as well. She held up the sign in front of her face, and then put it down to talk on the radio as she turned her back to me. She was embarrassed, helpless, guilty; she took this personally. Another few words on the radio. Although I couldn't hear what she said, her body language communicated... "Please give me back some control. Let my people go!" She didn't make eye contact until she flipped the sign to "slow" and waved me forward.

Her gestures showed that her mind was looking for an outlet, an immediate answer to "What do I do to get out of this uncomfortable situation?" Her solution was to use everything around her as a barrier between her and the people she presumed were judging her: the stop/slow sign, her radio, her helmet that partly shielded her eyes from ours, and her back.

You will commonly see behavior similar to this with a nervous speaker, who also presumes that everyone in the audience is judging him. In his mind, the barriers protect him from scrutiny: He stands behind the podium with the microphone angled to cover a portion of his face, and his hands lift the papers he's reading to further obscure him. If he's wearing glasses, the audience might see nothing but ears and hair the whole time he's presenting.

Mirroring

Mirroring can be a learned behavior, but, typically, it is nothing more than assimilation. Mirroring is a natural response to your culture; that's how we get to be homogeneous as a society. Mirroring the super-typical is a natural response to social norming.

We commonly get rewards—pay raises, compliments, and invitations to events—from other people in our culture when we behave similar to them. And when we don't become them, we are punished. High-pressure social norming is the *requirement* to mirror the behavior of others or face extremely unpleasant consequences. That's what happens in Stockholm syndrome. U.S. military basic training relies on a modified version with the Stockholm syndrome. The components are these: One man uses ritualistic rage to intimidate you, to control every moment of your life, and forces you to become like him. The new guy is like an ape thrown into a cage with 27 others who all know who the alpha is and what pleases him. You are the 28th ape who must try to figure that out so that the alpha doesn't tear your testicles off. So, you start to mimic him.

There is also intentional mirroring, or adaptational mirroring. That is part of manipulation, and in Part III I'll tell you how to use it so that it looks natural.

Rituals

Rituals range from formalized bits of ceremony to microcultural norms to personal habits. Sometimes we know their origins and purpose, and sometimes we don't have a clue, but we do them anyway. Why do most Americans put their knife down after cutting their meat, and then put their fork in the hand that held their knife? In the days of the American Revolution, the separatists and loyalists argued bitterly. These people were neighbors who shopped, worshipped, and ate together. So they developed a ritual that averted stabbings at the table and we follow it to this day: they put down the knife after they cut their meat.

If you are a non-Catholic and you have ever attended a Catholic Mass, you know you're an outsider because you don't know the rituals of the hundreds of other people in that church. On the other end of the spectrum, I know a skydiver who always puts her left glove on and then her right as she's preparing to jump; this has nothing to do with rituals of safety that her fellow skydivers follow. It's a personal superstition.

In the middle of the spectrum, you have cultural norms related to proximity to another person, signs of respect for people in authority, and so on. One arcane norm that relates to space, as well as eye contact, plays out in public bathrooms every day. In the average urinal in America—and this is not something that women personally witness—we follow the "urinal rules." Rule #1: Do not look down over the barrier. Rule #2: Conversation with strangers concurrently using the urinal is not acceptable. Rule #3: If you want to talk with the man you've spotted while you're both at the urinal—maybe you want to know where he got his tie—wait until you both get to the sink and you're washing your hands. Is this the same for all men? Of course not, but it is a valid generalization because it fits for a huge chunk of the population.

Two people in a relationship will commonly develop microcultural rituals to show affection, anger, boredom, and so on. When you extricate yourself from a long-term relationship, part of the baggage you take along is the signs and rituals that you developed in the context of that relationship. These may come back to haunt the next relationship.

In reading someone's body language, you will occasionally come across gestures that you will think must mean something, but, in fact, they may merely be personal rituals. What generally happens is that you repeat a gesture so frequently in private that it leaks into your public presentation. Maybe you pick at your front tooth when you're thinking. Chances are that you will be sitting in a meeting one day picking at your tooth. Other people may be completely distracted by your odd habit, but you won't even realize you're doing it.

Some gestures have taken on meaning through cultural context and you can only truly understand them as part of that culture. Then again, as advertising and media span the globe, some cultural gestures or icons have become ubiquitous and super-cultural: the name Coca-Cola , the word "okay," and the thumbs-up gesture.

Other very specific gesturing can result from a group's evolution, and this occurred to me as I attended a horse auction. Most new people are almost wooden the first few times they go to an auction such as this. They are afraid of signaling. A good auctioneer knows the itchy nose scratch from the bid nose scratch, though. They see the intensity of the gaze and contact made between the auctioneer and bidder.

In becoming a skilled practitioner of reading body language, you need to become the auctioneer. This means looking for the other pieces of body language when you see what looks like a gesture. Is there focus of energy? Does the person have eye contact? What does the rest of the body say? No single gesture or flinch can tell you something when it stands alone, unless it is a piece of symbolic language, such as the middle finger. Even when you see such a symbol, you must be like the auctioneer and say to yourself, "Does this person look like a seasoned auction attendee, or just someone here for a weekend of entertainment?"

The Holistic View: E in R.E.A.D.

Without the benefit of having you in a classroom, I needed to find different approaches to teach you how to view body language holistically. The results are two complementary systems of review: one for mood, and the other for posture. The latter is a version of what I teach military, law enforcement, and other students in security. The former is a new system I developed to give you a streamlined way to understand what the pieces probably mean when they come together. "Probably" refers to whether the actions come from the gut or from the brain of someone who knows how to manipulate body language. (There are not that many of us.) The mood system is a work in progress that I will continue to refine as I use it with students—and myself—in the upcoming years. As I said before, I am similar to Jane Goodall among the chimps, with one caveat: I am also a chimp.

C
H
A
P
T
E
R

5

Mood

This system offers a framework to determine what the body is saying overall. It structures your observations.

Only a delusional person wakes up in the morning and declares, "Today, I will demonstrate clearly what I am thinking through body language!" Most of what happens is hardwired. We are good at blocking portions of our body language but not good at seeing ourselves as we are. This is based partly on the fact that we respond to positive and negative feedback to create a repertoire that works for us socially, both consciously and subconsciously. Remember the key message of the culture chapter: Unless we are alpha, we are emulating the alpha and overlaying it to our own catalog of gestures to maintain identity while keeping alpha happy. Even if we are alpha, we must constantly be wary of challengers and adapt, lest she become alpha and we drop to typical.

When I look at someone from across the room, I get a sense of what is going on in that person's head. Until now, it was difficult for me to tell you how I knew. When asked how I could be so sure what a person's performance would be on the job, or how she might interact with other people, I would brush it off with, "It's my muse." By that I meant that I'd made my decision so quickly that I felt I couldn't take credit for deciding consciously.

This system codifies what my brain does for me in those circumstances, and the intent is that it will help your brain learn to do the same.

To begin, there are three parts to looking at the holistic body language of a person.

1. **Energy:** How lively is the person? Does she look tired or invigorated? Is it normal or abnormal? When I say "energy," I am talking from head to toe, and even more than that. Bill Clinton has energy that showed even after his heart surgery. If I were to see that energy fail, it indicates that something is going on in his head to cause a downward shift.

2. **Direction:** Is the energy this person displays freewheeling, all over the board? Is it sharply aimed at a common goal? Temper this perception with what is normal for the person. You cannot, for instance, look once at someone who is scatterbrained and assume there is a root cause other than genes.

3. **Focus:** Is the energy focused internally or externally? Is the person directed at getting away from something, or simply disconnected from those around him? This can tell us more about the mental state of someone than the other two combined.

These three, primary criteria form the foundation of this new system for looking holistically at a person. They serve as big-chunk categories in analyzing behavior. I'm going to wrap them in a simple label: mood indicators. Combined with the scalp-to-sole list and the checklist on posture that follows, you can get close to clarifying the meaning of a person's body language.

The concept is simple: Use the three elements to describe the overall effect that the scalp-to-sole elements present when they come together.

For example, energy is low or high. Direction answers the question: Are all of the arrows lined up? Is the person paying sharp attention to a person, place, or thing with all outward expression and the senses? Is all of that energy sharply directed at one target or scattered among several preoccupying factors?

Focus is either internal or external. It could be sharp or scattered relative to something apparent to the outside world, or the focus—sharp or scattered—could be on something inside his head.

The following table provides a sampling of moods or emotions and a profile of them according to energy, direction, and focus.

Mood	Energy	Direction	Focus
Confusion	Low	Scattered	Internal
Distraction	High	Scattered	Internal
Anger	High	Sharp	External
Joy	High	Sharp	External
Excitement	High	Scattered	Stimulus dependant
Interest	High	Sharp	External
Fear	High	Sharp	External
Secretiveness	Low	Sharp	External
Embarrassment	Low	Sharp	Internal

Confusion

Energy low, direction scattered, focus internal.

A great movie moment that shows confusion is Mel Gibson in *Braveheart* when his character, William Wallace, discovers that Robert the Bruce has betrayed him. Wallace's preoccupation moves deeper into the psyche—a depiction of internal focus. He seems so occupied that he may not even notice anything else. His mind has discovered something that threatens his very being, and that enemy has sapped his energy. There is suddenly an incongruity in his picture of the universe.

Distraction

Energy high, direction scattered, focus internal.

You wake up in the morning and know you will be late for work; you have too many things to do before you leave. You run around the house looking for keys, trying to remember what else you need to take with you. Nothing goes right.

People in this state may say they are confused, but the truth is, the mind has an overwhelming preoccupation: *I'm late*. This fixation prevents focus on anything else as long as the mind knows there is urgency at hand. Under these conditions, body language has no consistent direction, meaning the syntax of the body language is discordant, and not sending a unified signal.

Anger

Energy high, direction sharp, focus external.

Most people can recognize anger easily when it's openly expressed. What if the person masks it, though? Are there still tell-tale signs? By using a whole-body approach and narrowing to the differences between anger and distraction or anger and fear, for example, you can find the signs. Begin by understanding what picture the canvas presents, and then look at the individual colors—the hands, feet, eyes, lips, nose, and so on.

Anger involves an energy level so high that it seeps out, even when a person tries to mask it. The angry person has a consuming drive to deal with the cause. Direction is not an issue, either. This individual has unity of purpose in body and mind: eliminate the cause of his anger.

In men, the direction manifests itself in physical displays of aggression, whether overt or masked. In women, this demonstration can simply be a sharpening of the wit or more feminine behavior. The commonality is hyper-demonstrative gender behavior. Women rarely fistfight—they "catfight" instead. Similar to cats, they pose and growl a lot, often with little contact other than the swipe of a claw.

Angry men have a decidedly external focus, in some cases even to the detriment of the well-cultivated persona. The old Southern gentleman can, indeed, be pushed to beat your ass in the parking lot. In women, this focus is never quite so narrow until rage, the next level of intensity, enters the picture. If men are prepared for hand-to-hand combat early on, women are prepared to fence. Women will typically focus on the cause, while keeping in mind the preservation of species. By her very nature, a woman remains more cognitive than a man during times of anger, if not as in control. The root of this difference is the size of the amygdala, the brain structure associated with aggression. It's larger in men than in women, so while angry men move, angry women tend to observe and process.

Similar to the cat, the growling and hissing will result in action only in dire straits.

Joy

Energy high, direction sharp, focus external.

So far, joy looks identical to anger. Because of their identical profiles, they are both easy to identify. The physiological difference is what part of brain is engaged, and the emotional difference can be described in terms of magnetism: anger repels and joy attracts.

I describe joy as overwhelming happiness. One would only have to meet me to wonder why I would understand this concept. Joy is not a typical soldier trait. My Army buddies and I once played a horrible practical joke on a fellow soldier in my days at Arlington because we wanted to provoke this "unsoldierly" emotion. We copied this guy's numbers from a lottery ticket he left on a desk. Shortly after that, he came to ask if anyone knew the winning numbers. We sent him to the person he thought was the most credible guy in the unit, and this trusted source read off the numbers one by one. As the numbers matched he became progressively more excited. When he heard the last number, this balding, thick-waisted old soldier sprang into the air and kicked his feet like a boy. This reckless abandon of his personal image came crashing down when he looked into the next room where we were all in our own perverted demonstrations of joy.

Depending on culture, people display high energy differently. For instance, an acceptable level of energy associated with joy in a young woman will elicit stares when used by a middle-aged man.

When we sign a contract for a new publishing project, Maryann raises her hands past the shoulder and has a gleeful look on her face, with lots of energy bubbling to the highest parts of her body. I, on the other hand, smile. It is a very large smile and my body becomes more animated, but I don't "do" gleeful. What is the difference, aside from the impact of ovaries and testes? Living with the military since the age of 14, and raised by Southern parents. Do we start to see the impact of layers of culture, subculture, and sex on a simple expression of joy? How does a child's energy level differ before he understands men generally do not flit about?

Similar to a person demonstrating anger, a person demonstrating joy stays focused on the cause. Direction of energy is unilateral. The only additional factor is whether the joy relates to something present or a past occurrence that has just come to the person's attention. Watch a person who has just learned of great news from a letter. Does she hold the letter as a relic in this ritual of celebration, or discard it and dance around? She holds on to it, most likely. When a person learns joy-causing news over the phone, all energy goes into the conversation. Even the eyes may find their way toward the phone. Every ounce of the person's being is concentrated on what she perceives as the source.

Again, similar to anger, the initial external focus can shift to the inside. In joy, it happens as the person relishes the impact of the profound event on his life: The new book contract causes a celebration, but the long-term effect of having a greater sense of purpose moves the joy inward. The focus may go strictly internal as the person tries to sustain the feeling of euphoria by thinking of all the spillover effects of the good news.

Excitement

Energy high, direction scattered, focus stimulus dependent.

Arguably, excitement is a category under which many of the other moods can fall. For a moment, suspend disbelief and imagine that excitement is only a single mood not caused by anger, joy, and so on. It's just a feeling that comes from your synapses firing.

As the happy-excited person comes to life, his center of gravity seems to rise, as though the weight of years is leaving. His face lights up and he seems desperate to communicate. This kind of excitement creates a youthful appearance even in the elderly, as the posture becomes more erect and pace of movement increases. Think of a child at Christmas, or even an adult at Christmas who anticipates receiving or giving the perfect gift.

Excitement could also stem from anxiety, aggravation, or a number of other negatives. The face would show the big distinctions, but the body will show similarities to that of the happy-excited person, specifically, signs of increased animation.

All of that energy needs to go somewhere. If the person is in the presence of others and the cause of the excitement is open for public discussion, the person will want to share. She'll probably lock on to any keyword in the conversation that can steer it back to the subject of her excitement. If the cause of it is not open for discussion—an illicit affair at the office—she will leak her feelings when oblique references to the subject come up. Whether you can see the source of the excitement or not, you can easily see the aura caused by the bouncing energy. For this reason, few people can keep a secret that affects their own lives.

Although the focus depends on what causes the excitement, it's almost always external. When excitement has an element of secretiveness, as in the case of an illicit affair, this focus will vacillate. But put her source of excitement in the room and, regardless of where her eyes are, her focus will be on that person. To anyone even mildly astute, it creates a stream of energy that signals "something's going on." The gossip columns call it "sparks flying." This is one reason why people know about an affair before the spouse who's wronged. The focus is external, so the energy comes out.

Think of a child the first time she sees Santa—full of excitement, but conflicted about whether it's good or bad excitement. She knows he gives gifts, but that laugh sounds fake. Maybe he *eats* kids after he gives them gifts! After embracing a benevolent Santa, she imagines the possibilities of all he will give her; later when she thinks of him, her focus is internal. On Christmas night when she hears a sleigh bell ring, though, all of her energy turns externally to the old fat man in the red suit.

Interest

Energy high, direction sharp, focus external.

Back to the anger and joy profile. Full-blown curiosity can power the body as much as food. Think of an inquisitive toddler who cannot be distracted from tearing apart a new gift to see what's inside. Actually, that's a boy toddler; a girl with just as much interest in the gift is likely to explore its facets more cautiously and ask a lot of whys and hows. Regardless of the approach, all energy is directed at the object of their interest. The movie *2001: A Space Odyssey* provides a perfect example of this in the opening scene, where the primates are obsessed with the obelisk. Any thought of self comes after "What the heck is this?" Or in the case of males, "Should I kill, eat, or breed this?"

In males, the predisposition toward action as part of satisfying curiosity keeps us externally focused, often without concept of self or personal limitations. As part of our "people watching" for this book, we looked at little boys and girls on vacation with their parents in Estes Park, Colorado. This may not be a statistically valid assertion, but based on our observations, it sure is obvious: Little boys run onto things and into things and around things with reckless abandon. Little girls almost never do that. This is likely a response to high testosterone doses in the womb. I think that this natural inclination for action has served males primates well from an evolutionary point of view. The weaker male can pass his genes on to the object of his affection without regard for survival of the self if he acts more quickly. The alpha need not fear harm and can pass his genes without regard for personal injury. One has only to know a male child in his late teens to see this ape behavior in action.

Fear

Energy high, direction sharp, focus external.

If interest causes us to override our natural instincts to pull back, fear is the sudden reminder that we must do it. Fear arouses tremendous energy in preparation for action. When I was 8, I was trick-or-treating with my 4-year-old brother, my 6-year-old sister, and my 3-year-old cousin. We walked onto a porch and a man with a bloody stump for a head answered the door. Even a discerning 8-year-old did not recognize the stump as a pork chop sitting on top of a man's shirt. In total terror, I dove off the 3-foot-high porch and screamed to my little brother to run. He was well ahead of me. My sister, holding the hand of my toddler cousin, dragged him down the street while he screamed for her to run faster. In those days, I thought her hand wouldn't let go of him because it was paralyzed in fear. Today I believe her action was a standard female response to terror: save the baby.

Every one of us kids sharply directed our energy at getting the hell out of there. That's how fear operates; whether or not the direction is ideal, it is aimed at something particular. The energy is typically balled up in fear awaiting a release command from the limbic brain to fight, flee, or freeze, or in the case of women, a combination of actions. In all of these cases, though, the energy is unidirectional and prepared, and the focus is external. Eyes dilate to take in as much data as possible about the source of the fear. Then the body either turns away from the source, or toward the object to take a second look at the threat and determine a course of action. When the threat becomes omnipresent and overwhelming, a man takes action. This threshold for what is omnipresent varies from man to man.

However, a woman's external focus may be split between the threat and the object of her protection. For this reason, female prey will sometimes immediately attack a predator rather than run from it. These females don't want to leave their young as an appetizer, so they fight. In humans, the response is not as predictable, because females have a much better developed brain and a larger catalog of options than her quadriped counterparts.

Secretiveness

Energy low, direction sharp, focus external.

When someone is trying to hide something, elements of the other moods will creep in. Is she excited because it is a surprise party? Afraid because it is an affair? Trying to hide the fact he is interested in something you are carrying or reading? In fact, you might see overlap in nearly all of the moods described here, primarily because secretiveness needs a root, emotional cause.

An attempt to be secretive is a conscious effort. As such, you have to keep energy low, stay directed, and maintain an external focus or you'll give yourself away. At the same time, most humans are not aware of the layers of moods they have, so maintaining absolute control over these three elements is beyond most people's ability. In order to know what the person is hiding, you will have to work at uncovering the layers.

Here's an important irony that will help you: by its very nature, hiding something is energy intensive. Have you ever tried to keep a secret when someone is prodding? This energy is constantly trying to go somewhere, and as a consequence, tends to leak out in odd and visible ways. The more polished among us find successful routines to redirect this energy. Through experimentation, we learn what works, such as playing on our sexuality or even pretending to be dimwitted to divert suspicion from our real intent.

Secretiveness, therefore, is characterized by large amounts of contained energy. Look for adaptors, the gestures of energy displacement. There is a direct relationship between the amount of energy someone is fighting to hold in or displace, and the significance of the secret.

When obsessed with a singular issue, a person has single direction; this is especially true with secretiveness. Everything in the person's mind revolves around the importance of covering tracks and preventing discovery. That plays out in clues. For example, just as a child obsessed with Santa turns every conversation to Santa, a secretly cheating spouse will take odd turns in conversation to reference or avoid reference to infidelity. When referencing infidelity, she is likely testing the water for how he feels about it or what he knows. When avoiding, she knows how he will react and wants to stay away at all costs from the topic. Either will create a contrived sort of division of the conversation. It reminds me of a story I heard from someone learning to drive a race car. The instructor said, "Don't look at the wall or you'll hit it." So what do most people do. They look at the wall. It's just human nature.

Secretive people who are skillful maintain strict external focus. They want to stay away from too much of what is in their own heads—they don't want to hit the wall—and they want to focus on the other person's conversation. First of all, this allows him an opportunity to discover what the other knows and side-step discovery. People transmit their own thoughts when speaking, even when asking a question. Secondly, no one likes to keep a secret all to himself, so listening carefully might help him find a confidant.

Embarrassment

Energy low; direction sharp, focus internal.

Almost all grand embarrassment is preceded by secretiveness. This is not the momentary kind that comes from farting in public. Grand embarrassment can arise from displaced expectations all the way up to discovery of the family skeletons.

Embarrassed people typically do not know what to do with this sudden, unexpected flow of energy. They know what caused the embarrassment and sharply direct their attention on it. They don't know where to put all of the energy it provoked, though, so it often comes boomeranging back at them. Whether embarrassment becomes anger, excitement, joy, or confusion, all are related to how the person deals with directing the energy and whether the focus becomes internal or external. This will be largely culture-dependant.

Direction in embarrassment is unilateral. All arrows are lined with the course of action the person decides to take to escape the cause, even though displaced expectation makes the person seem distracted for a moment. An average American called to speak in front of a crowd will begin to use this direction of energy to create barriers and use adaptors to comfort himself. This same person called a liar in public may have an extremely different, secondary reaction: one that includes discrediting the accuser. The course of action depends upon whether this highly directed energy is focused internally or externally.

Where a person focuses energy in embarrassment is largely cultural. When I say culture, I mean from microculture through superculture. In May 1991, Queen Elizabeth paid a visit to the Marshall

Heights Community Development Organization, a subsidized housing project in Washington, D.C. Resident Alice Frazier greeted Her Majesty with a bear hug, which caused a mixture of abject embarrassment and shock on the part of former First Lady Barbara Bush, the D.C. mayor, and the secretary of housing and urban development. In fact, the only people who didn't seem to be bothered by the egregious breach of protocol were Mrs. Frazier and the queen.

The more comfortable a person is with an experience, no matter how unusual, the more likely a person will handle the embarrassing moment with tact, grace, and will be able to internalize the energy.

Experiment with this system of codifying the three main traits of human moods. Make your own table and create profiles for other emotional states as well, for honing your "review" skills.

Expand the system and make it your own. What other criteria might you add? How about dress? Is it even possible for the Pope to show absolute joy—an explosion of energy—while he's wearing his mitre and pallium, and carrying the pastoral staff? This is not only a matter of the physical limitations of the clothing, but also the gravity of the office represented by the clothing.

Does the role you play in life affect your expressions of moods? Surely the queen would have reacted differently to the hugger if she were not practiced in controlling her state. Is there likely a difference in energy level and focus as we shift from role to role in our daily lives? Most humans have a thick, layered skin of diversions and disguises when it comes to emotions; this system is just one more way to skin the monkey.

Posture

Culture profoundly affects posture. From the smallest group to the largest, you need to consider influences on openness, energy, flexibility, and movements—all elements of posture.

This gives you the basic model for how I will analyze posture to further develop your holistic view of body language. Each of these will play a part in what the person is conveying, intentionally or unintentionally, and each will reflect cultural influences.

What passes for good posture among average Americans would cause swift and severe punishment for any member of the United States Marine Corps. I started my career in the military as a short, 14-year-old junior ROTC (Reserve Officers' Training Corps) student. I was cajoled, ridiculed, and taught to stand like a soldier before most people ever consider joining the Army. Prepared for basic training and skilled in drills and ceremony, I felt ready for the rest of my Army career—at least the marching part. Five years later, I was assigned to the Old Guard, one of the oldest and most respected Infantry Regiments in the United States Army. Among other things, the Old Guard protects the Tomb of the Unknowns at Arlington National Cemetery and has a prominent role in burials at the cemetery. I soon realized my idea of good military posture fell short of the standards achieved by seasoned members of the Old Guard. Years later in a military intelligence unit, a major remarked he could tell I had been an Old Guard member by my ladder-straight back. The Old Guard microculture and the microculture that is military intelligence had very different takes on "military posture." Nevertheless, they seemed quite similar when I had exposure to non-American military units.

On one of my night guard shifts during Operation Desert Storm, I saw the effect of our U.S. military culture starkly. With night vision goggles, the world takes on a green glow that allows you to see detail relatively well up close, but poorly at distance. We were attached to the Kuwaiti brigade in an advisory role. I commented to the fellow soldier on guard at the time how easy it is to pick an American by posture. We joked that it made the Iraqi snipers' target acquisition much easier. The reason was simple: American soldiers had a very different cultural concept of time, mission, and focus that surfaced in their posture. Many of the Kuwaitis fighting to free their homeland were expatriate college students who returned to fight for the liberation of Kuwait. The culture of Kuwait places little value on promptness and it shows in the gait of the people. The fact that they were not military and non-Americans affected how straight each stood, where they directed their gaze, and so on. If many Americans have a tendency to stroll, most Arabs take it to new levels.

Openness

I will look at "closed" before "open" to engender your perspective on the topic.

When you started reading this book, one of your suppositions was likely that crossed arms serve as a defense, or meant that someone wanted to close you out. Did someone tell you that's what it meant, or did you feel it? Crossed arms are, in fact, one way that a person can block you out, but it can also signal fear, cold, confidence, arrogance, hiding a fat belly, and much more depending on context. Look at the photo with my bio on the back cover— what does it mean? More importantly than what it means in this case is the effect I am after: a jaundiced eye projecting mistrust. Never mind the fact that I was thinking what a nice job the photographer, Mr. Dougherty, was doing. This closed arm posture hides all of that and sends a different signal. Knowledge similar to this is important in review, but even more so in using these tools offensively.

Other ways of blocking include closing the elbows to the side, tightly buttoning clothing, barricading oneself behind a holy symbol such as a cross, and turning to oblique angles. Americans typically think that facing a person straight on while talking signifies honesty. Ironically, given a choice, two American men will probably not sit directly facing each other. Most will choose to sit at oblique angles. It is a subconscious way that men convey they do not wish to engage in confrontation. If you think in terms of the apes, facing directly into the eyes of the alpha will likely result, at the very least, in a demonstration of dominance. So, is this natural preference to sit at an angle an echo of the ape in us? Think of the last time you saw two American men in an altercation. Inevitably, the two square off, face to face; the implication is that angled posture is much friendlier. In contrast to this, it is not unusual to see two Arab men nearly touching faces and square-on discussing details of the weekend plans. If you're a man, take a minute and think about your own posture vis-á-vis other men of your own culture. If you're a woman, think about how you convey openness. It's generally in the same way that men display confrontation—face to face.

Exercise

Look in the mirror. Place your elbows close to your sides and raise your palms as if you are helpless. Now do the same gesture, but raise the elbows from the body. Which seems protected? Which seems genuine? Traditionally, open arms are viewed as welcome. This closed-to-the-sides posture showing vulnerability is instinctively distrusted by every one of my students. Most cannot tell you why. Now you know.

Our nature is to demonstrate how open we are to acquaintances, whether new or old. Warm and open take on different appearances in different cultures, but all have one thing in common: displaying vulnerability to show openness.

The military salute is the most formal of greetings, a way to show servitude to superiors. A rigid and formalized gesture, it presents the right hand to the brow. Numerous theories try to explain why this developed, from a knight opening his visor to show his face, to the exposure of a hand without a weapon. The meaning is still the same: "I am raising my primary weapon into a nonready position, to show servitude."

The American handshake carries a related meaning: "I am offering you my primary weapon and I would like yours in exchange." The Asian bow: "I am lowering my unprotected skull." How much more open, that is, vulnerable, can a human get? These actions capture the essence of why openness is so important in communication. Humans are a perceptive lot even when their culture dulls the senses.

Openness can come from relative position as well. If I stand at a somewhat oblique angle to another American man, he will perceive it as open. If I turn to face him head-on, I usually notice he will shift to keep this position less confrontational. By oblique I do not mean a T-formation. If I do move to the T and close in on the person's dominant hand, he will perceive that as a threat, too. Try it if you doubt me. Add to that squared shoulders as you talk. Do you see a difference? Experiment with someone you know, not someone you've just met in an elevator.

Clothing can demonstrate openness as well. When John Mark Karr confessed to killing JonBenét Ramsey, he wore his collar buttoned to the top. Oddly enough, the first question thrown at me on CNN that night related to his tightly buttoned collar. This is a piece of body language that probably strikes many people as closed at first glance. I avoided the question, by the way, because I did not know whether it was his norm; I do not like to think in absolutes and did not want to be painted into that corner. Karr's microculture could play a part in his dressing that way. But if that is not his norm, buttoning his collar to the top is, in fact, a barrier.

Openness, or lack thereof, can also be demonstrated by barriering with objects or with natural tools: hands, ankles, knees, or even fingers. Objects can make a person feel safer—a rolled magazine, a purse, a laser pointer, a cell phone. Look for use of these tools not as a screen to hide body language physically, but a way to divert energy away from the face and body. Repeated or consistent use of them as barriers in a conversation probably means you should look beyond them to find nervousness, anger, disgust, or embarrassment. In an office, of course, the most common barrier is a person's desk.

In class, I flash a picture of several people on the screen, and after a split second, ask, "Who do you trust?" Inevitably, the person they trust least is the one who looks the most closed. Whether it is because of dress that is traditionally non-Western, or clothes that cover more of the person than most Americans are accustomed to seeing, the formula becomes: the more hidden, the less trustworthy. Would growing up in Saudi Arabia change this? Highly likely.

Where you put your hands and how closed you sit or stand will affect how trusted you are. I have intentionally modified my posture during a job interview to see how the interviewer would react. The more I rounded my upper body and hid my hands—closed signs that represent vulnerability—the more probing he became.

Energy

Energy level tells more about what is going on in the head than the body.

The Army required a command presence during nonduty hours, so one person was designated to sit at a desk anytime the commanding officer was not present. At the lower levels, the title was CQ (charge of quarters), and higher up, SDNCO (staff duty noncommissioned officer). During the week, this started after the duty day and ran through the beginning of the next day. On weekends, it was a 24-hour duty. In either case, the person was awake for more than 24 hours. I served as CQ on the Friday before I bought my first horse. My energy level was through the floor until I got to the stable. I remember spending hours at the stable awake and fully charged up. Why? The brain creates energy for the body.

How well do you sleep the night before a big trip? How about the night before the first day of a new job? This energy affects posture more than facial expression. I can look like hell in the face from lack of sleep, but move around as though I am myself and appear to be fine.

The energy I am talking about here is not the bubbly little kid kind, which I do cover in the section on movement. This is energy to the joints that gives you the impression the person's back is strong and under control *versus* sloppy and sagging. Depression and a sense of failure manifest themselves in lack of energy to the joints. The back is similar to a suspension bridge and all of those cables need energy to stay taut. When the energy subsides, the posture droops.

As you learn about baselining in Chapter 7, you will see how important this criterion becomes in reading an individual's body language. Even if a person's normal posture is not up to Old Guard standards, you can tell when his energy level changes, and move toward conclusions about his emotional and mental state.

Flexibility

Any personal trainer or physical therapist will harp on the benefits of flexibility, but my definition is a little different from theirs. By flexibility I refer to rounded movements—swivels, slumps, bends at the joints, and so on—as opposed to movements with a degree of rigidity. Posture with square corners—shoulders back, feet planted firmly beneath—is a more male, and less flexible, posture. Rounded shoulders and feet that shift weight from one side to another is typically more female and seen as feminine. The gender differences between these postures come out of anatomical differences, which also tend to make women more flexible in the conventional sense used by trainers and therapists.

Men typically have broader, more developed shoulders, and a narrower pelvis with legs closely set. This creates an image that is triangular and has harsher angles than a woman's body. The angles translate to straighter movement and a squarer gait. Men walk and move in a straight line very efficiently. This squared off movement will often give away even the well-practiced transgender females and drag queens who don't have a woman's broad-set hips and their natural predisposition toward lateral, fluid movement. Movement of men's arms looks as though it originates from above, but when a woman moves her arms, it's not as if it is dangling as much as it is sweeping from below. Add to this the fact that muscles attach at different points on the frame and you get a naturally more rounded look in women than men. Sure, this can be disguised, hidden, or changed with clothing, weight, surgery, exercise, or training, but no matter how you slice it, all these elements do is decorate the frame, not alter it.

As a reminder, this discussion is not about men and women having equal competence in certain sports and other physical challenges. These distinctions are only important in discussing posture as it relates to body language.

With gender being a shifting concept in our culture, I should make one quick note here. Anger will move you closer to the behavior of the gender with which you identify. Women will instinctively express their femininity, rounding the shoulders and shifting the center of gravity. Very effeminate men will become more demonstratively feminine.

Men and more masculine women will make themselves squarer and blocky in their movements. When people become enraged, the animal takes over. I have little experience to define how effeminate men or masculine women behave in rage.

One constant is that when people become emotionally tender, all of us become more rounded. Go to a bar, or any place you can watch people trying to make a connection. In a bar, the men will be very masculine, square standing, and using straight-line movement until they pass a point at which bonding begins. At that point, the speed of behavior slows and the man's movement and posture will start to round. The same is true for sadness and depression. Watch men become softer as these emotions hit.

Movement

Every subculture of which you are a part will affect how you move. Professional dancers will show traces of training in daily movement. Police officers responsible for crowd control will also have residual movement patterns. Everything we do, whether as hobby or profession, leaves muscle memory on our bodies. In this section, I will give you an overview of movement. An entire book could be dedicated to reading the body language of movement and ritual, so consider this simply an introduction to gait, center of gravity, and overall body movement.

Gait

"Put some pep in your step" is a military expression that actually means something specific. Drill sergeants will use this cliché when trying to turn average Americans into marching soldiers. The normal marching gait is called quick-time. A cadence of 120 steps per minute, a stride of 30 inches heel to toe, and prescribed arm movement of 9 inches to the front and 6 inches to the rear is the prescribed gait for an American soldier while marching. A drill instructor drums the proper lilt, or spring, to the military marching step into your head with "stop bee bopping" or some other cliché to remind you that marching leaves no room for creativity. Just do what you are told by the person calling the commands. When I say that culture has a pronounced impact on gait, think about marching like that almost every day for 15 years and you have the most extreme example I can think of. Muscle memory from that repeated experience will forever change the way you walk.

I will use these components to analyze gait: speed, stride, lilt, and focus.

Speed

Speed correlates to a sense of urgency. It's funny to see a man who has never run a day in his life struggling to make his way at high-speed through the airport. Maybe airport security should have a "lumbering ape" alert so people can drag their children to safety. The running man who "never" runs has no muscle memory to support that speed, so even without a baseline, you can determine with certainty that his emotional state is "urgency." While speed can be achieved by simply lengthening the stride, most people do not have the option of lengthening stride enough to fulfill this sense of urgency.

Contrast this with my running through the airport. I run on a regular basis and never walk the stairs, unless it is in a setting where people would find running the steps strange or threatening. It rarely looks out of place for me to do it and I rarely get a second glance because there is a congruity between my pace and my muscle memory.

Stride

Most people have a natural stride or length of step that falls somewhere around the 30-inch range (heel to toe) that the Army dictates for marching. Height and length of limbs dictate this, of course, as well as travel companions.

With a 36-inch inseam and wearing boots, I have long legs; Maryann doesn't. When we launched *How to Spot a Liar* at the Capitol in Washington, D.C., we were asked to meet with a news team from Channel 9. A little confusion about the exact location sent us several blocks away from the actual rendezvous point. When we called and found out we needed to travel several blocks, I did not change my speed, but simply lengthened my stride to what is normal for me. Maryann had no more length in her stride, so her only option was to speed; in fact, every five to seven steps she would jog a few steps in her heels. It's a fond memory because it added texture to the day (and her heels no doubt added texture to the grounds on the West lawn of the Capitol).

This shortening or lengthening of stride will tell you a bit about the urgency and intent of the person in the situation. In this case, the urgency and intent were clear. Maryann and I were carrying on a civil conversation, so why would I walk her into the ground unless we were in a hurry to get somewhere? Change the picture a bit. What if we were both walking the same pace, but Maryann was complaining about something I'd done? The message of my body language then changes to "I'm getting away from you."

Lilt

A man headed for the gas chamber is not likely to do so with spring in his step. The opposite is true when someone is walking on stage for well-deserved recognition. Even an introvert will tele-graph his thoughts when being recognized for brilliance by a bounce in his step. I often sit in the airport sorting who is on business travel and who is traveling for fun simply by watching the bounce in a person's step. I will often ask the person when I eventually sit down next to him, and have rarely been wrong. The exception is the new road warrior who still thinks it is sexy to jump on an airplane for business.

Focus

Have you ever been behind (or maybe you are part of) an old couple in an automobile just watching the cows eat grass? Then you know where I'm going with the focus piece.

Let's go back to the airport, where you can tell the people who do not travel often. The adventure is the trip, not the destination. They clog the moving sidewalks, miss moving up in line when it's their turn, and just generally do not seem to notice what is going on around them. The reason is focus. The seasoned traveler sees the security line, airport, and check-in as hindrances to his eventual goal. He is going somewhere to do something and the result is a focus of movement.

Center of gravity

Personal trainers and physical therapists have a specific physiological meaning for "center of gravity." This is my own creation and definition for center of gravity. I use the phrase to mean the center of a person's movement, where the energy is focused. Elements such as gender, weight, and culture play into this and simple observation has taught me to recognize it.

When was the last time you saw a young man wandering aimlessly and looking unhappy? Though thin and light on his feet, his energy has sunken to a point well below his face. An idiom such as "down in the dumps" captures the look. Men who walk solidly and land squarely on the heels of their feet appear grounded. Higher, more expressive energy centered around the upper body appears more feminine. The expression "light in the loafers" to describe an effeminate male refers to this look. All of these points of focus for energy play into my view of the person's center of gravity.

A young American man will typically have a center of gravity that is high and somewhere around the chest. Contrast this to an American woman who will have a center of gravity somewhat lower-typically between solar plexus and hips. Gymnastics equipment and events are one example in which center of gravity plays a key role in the design: men do parallel bars and rings to take advantage of upper body strength; women do uneven parallel bars and balance beam to exploit the athletic advantages of their lower center of gravity. This affects walking and other common movements in a number of ways.

As a typical American man moves, he will catch his weight on his heels and roll forward to the balls of his feet. His shoulders are the eye-catching part of his movement; his hips are typically squared. When an American woman walks, she is likely to catch her weight somewhere forward of the heel; many women actually walk on the balls of their feet. Her hips are the eye-catching part of her movement. While she may pose her shoulders due to good posture or to give a better look at her assets, those gestures reflect intention, not an anatomical predisposition.

Exercise

For a woman: Walk with your shoulders squared and land on your heels, roll your weight to the balls of your feet with your hips square and no swish. How does that feel? Even if you think yourself a bit masculine, the movements are likely uncomfortable physically, because your hips are poorly placed on the pelvis for this movement. Did you notice how little you use your shoulders? Now watch other women try this and contrast with what you see in men.

For a man: Raise the weight from your heels and move it forward to the center or balls of your feet. Lead with your hips and slightly sway as you walk. Try not to engage your shoulders in a swagger. (I have made the men's test easier because our brains work better with finite tasks.) What did you find? Does the term "light in the loafers" come to mind?

As we age and add weight, the center of gravity usually heads south. Nature takes away the squareness of most men through muscle atrophy and padding at the mid-section. An old Southernism calls this "furniture disease"—when your chest falls into your drawers. Men start to lose muscle mass in the chest and shoulders; what you get is a shrunken, droopy upper body, thickened waist, and flabby behind. Oh, but chances are good he walks the same—heel-toe-heel-toe—because of his muscle memory. Now, however, the extra weight on his frame striking the heels jars his compressing spine, so he shifts forward of the heel. The once tall-standing, high-center-of-gravity man now pitches forward when he walks. His square posture is more rounded and he looks centered closer to the solar plexus or hips. His gait and appearance has become more feminine with age. Reading the posture portion of his body language must take this into consideration. With many older men, you will need to pay attention to how they compensate for the changes.

Take John Wayne. How did he maintain his image of a super-masculine man until he died at the age of 72? Did his weight shift to his drawers? If you look at him in *Stagecoach* (1939) and again in *True Grit* (1969), which he filmed 10 years before he died, he did become a different kind of manly man. His shoulders were rounded and failing in *True Grit*, and he had a large gut. He wears the well-designed Hollywood trappings of a cowboy to help hide this, though. The biggest thing that kept him from looking similar to Elmer Fudd was his gait. John Wayne had a unique sideways gait that never landed him on his heels, so little changed. Faithful audiences had no perception of the shift in his center of gravity and he still looked masculine.

Knowing what you know now, however, go back and watch *Stagecoach* and *True Grit* and compare Wayne's center of gravity in them.

Is age the only thing that changes our center of gravity?

 ## Exercises

1. Walk along at your normal gait and pace.

Now remember the last deeply emotional experience you had. A good chewing from the boss? A disappointing date? Failing a test? Pay attention to your center of gravity. Your head likely went down and to the right in response to emotion. When you carry around 20 pounds of dead weight in the form of your head and change its position relative to the body, everything has to accommodate it. It is simple mechanics.

2. Sadness and the darker emotions will drop your center of gravity and instantly age your movement, but lighter emotions will raise your center of gravity. Hold back on something exciting you want to share with someone until the last possible minute. Tune into your own body language as you move toward that person physically, with the intent of connecting with him emotionally. If you are middle-aged or older, you will feel

youth come back to your body as your exuberance causes you to pick up your step and move more nimbly to get there.

Overall movement

Is boundless activity or serenity more associated with the "ideal" in your culture? Do you want your children to bounce around and climb things, or to learn quickly to control and focus their energy?

In the United States, when a man enters a room, he will be perceived as in control and powerful if he is calm. There is a caveat: if he stands for too long with no contact with others, he becomes an outsider. Low levels of movement, with hands controlled and decisive at or around waist-level, are viewed as masculine in our northern European-descended culture. This same level of inactivity may be seen as odd coming from a woman.

Contrast this behavior with those of Mediterranean and Latin descent in the United States—Italians, Hispanics, Greeks, Turks, and so on. These cultures all use the hands demonstratively as part of normal illustration. The elbows may even rise close to shoulder level in men of these cultures. People with my military background see this kind of gesturing as hot-tempered, too emotionally involved. Let's get some perspective on this, though: Germanics and Brits are more the exception to body language than the norm in humankind. The waist-high, controlled gestures probably seem rather lame and uncommitted to many people around the world.

Overall movement is affected by several factors: some biological, some cultural, and some part of microculture so obscure that one can only wonder where they come from. I have tremendous amounts of energy and that energy needs to go somewhere. As a child I flitted about and was highly energetic, bordering on what would now be called hyperactive. A well-placed paddle across the rear end a few times in the second grade taught me to keep my butt on the seat. With time, I realized most men do not flit about. I also realized I could turn that tremendous energy into mental energy to observe people and learn. The energy still leaks from my mouth though, and I often talk much more than an average American man.

When I am agitated and not speaking, I start to move my hands or feet, and I look as though I am ready to jump into the conversation. In fact, I may interject words. This is a learned part of co-instructing; it means I think my opinion has value at that moment and I sometimes interject in ways that are not normal for most people. This is a cultural norm of teaching. My energy leaks significantly if I am in a room where this is not acceptable. Does my energy look similar to that of a Latino man who is agitated? No. It is much more contained, but if you look closely, you can still see the child that became me.

In reading overall movement, look for energy that is contained and leaking from somewhere else. The scene in *The Bird Cage* in which Robin Williams tries to contain his flamboyant partner's (Nathan Lane) behavior by putting him in a suit and teaching him to "walk like a man" provides an extreme example of that.

Application

I could have started this book with the holistic chapter, but that would have skewed your vision of the smaller, more subtle signals people send. Rather than that quick-fix approach to reading body language, I've helped you develop an eye for reviewing the pieces of body language and speculating about what they could mean. You have practiced your review skills to the point that you can now see similarities and differences. And you understand that sometimes people scratch their nose because it itches.

Using the holistic approach with those basics to better understand the overall person now allows you to create categories of moods. The large-chunk pieces allow you to overlay the smaller, subtler actions you've examined and to notice what stands out. When your eyes notice a nuance that has more meaning than the collection of individual actions, you have reached the "E" in R.E.A.D.

So now, I want you to start the evaluation process. You will move from "What is in the picture from scalp to sole?" to "What is in the picture from scalp to sole that is unusual or telling?" And "How can I know its true meaning?"

Example

I have a project that is falling behind, but I manage to keep my fingers in the dam to prevent catastrophe. I watch the boss come in Friday morning. He walks intently, his gait faster than normal. As he approaches the office, he is holding his coffee with both hands and only releases to rub his forehead once. His overall movement is contained, but there is a nervous energy—choppier than normal. As he passes my door, he glances at his shoes. Should I be concerned? If so, why?

Nothing occurs in a vacuum, so ask yourself what real-life elements would play in here. Paranoid delusions aside, you might evaluate the situation like this:

⇒ The faster-than-normal gate with barriering projects a desire to minimize exposure time.

⇒ The jerky movement indicates a preoccupied mind.

⇒ The fact that he averted his gaze down could be outright guilt.

Your interpretation at this point is that maybe you should be concerned. After all, Friday in the United States is the most popular day to terminate employees for non-performance. What you have done in this situation is review all of the body language and apply what you know about the boss's norms, and then look for the pieces that stand out to evaluate his body language. You added to that a factor that colors the context—something I will go into more in Chapter 7.

Up to now, I have given you overall tools for absorbing information about other people. I did not have to teach you to evaluate—you taught yourself the "E." You are now noticing the subtleties of a person's communication style and are almost ready to move on. Almost. First, you need to know what causes this information to be tainted.

Filters: Sex and Other Misconceptions

A good interrogator is always hedging bets, seeing how much he can get away with. The techniques he uses center on his ability to manipulate your filters—gender-related traits, cultural factors, and projections.

When I'm trying to build rapport with a mature Arab man in interrogation, I begin with the likelihood that he has a son, and that his son is the light of his life. So I may begin with, "Your oldest child, your son...." He will not say, "No, my daughter." It will not happen. Even if he has a daughter that is his oldest child, he would not admit that to an Anglo. And then I would refer to the son by one of the popular names for an oldest male and have roughly a 40 percent chance of getting it right. By this time, I've used his own filters to convince him that I know more about him than I actually do.

C
H
A
P
T
E
R

6

A fortune teller without any special powers, except of the knowl-edge of communication filters, will be able to do the same thing. You walk away $100 poorer, convinced that she saw into your past: therefore, she must know something about your future.

If I know you spent the first 20 years of your life in upstate New York, with no heavy ethnic orientation, I can make certain assumptions about your body language. The kind of movements you make will be somewhat at odds with what is normal and acceptable for someone from the backwoods of Georgia. The cadence of your speech, word choices, and other aspects of your verbal, vocal, and non-verbal communication will help me profile you.

Now turn around all of these things I've said about filters and focus on yourself. If you can't identify your own filters, recognize how they affect your view of others, or learn to control them, your ability to read someone else's body language will be impaired. Assumptions, projections, and biases can clog your ability to sense and intuit information about someone.

Gender

Men and women can more easily understand each other than act similar to each other. That said, understanding each other is far from easy. The biological and anatomical differences that influence behavior also switch on powerful filters that make it hard for us to eliminate biases we have about the opposite sex. In briefly reviewing those differences, I want to center your attention on both. Why gender-related filters have such control over our thinking and how they operate, and how men and women differ in their body language.

The discussion starts with the impact of the primary sex organs, which do not only affect how we see our identity, but they also affect how we think, move, and live. This is mainly through the introduction of hormones to our systems, which starts in the womb. Whether we want to admit it or not, we all start as female. If doses of testosterone later flood the fetus, the tissue that would have become an ovary can descend to become a testicle. Some researchers have documented that the length of man's or woman's ring finger in comparison to the index finger will tell you how much testosterone a person was exposed to as a fetus. People with longer ring fingers theoretically were exposed to more testosterone in the womb than others.

In my younger, higher risk-taking days, a female interrogator once told me that I suffered from testosterone poisoning. The implications are clear. Whether you measure it in broken bones or the cost of car insurance, testosterone drives young males to take more physical risks than young females. Jim McCormick, whose expertise as a speaker, author, and coach is risk-taking, conducted a study related to the risk inclination of various populations:

> My research shows that men's and women's inclination to take social and creative risks are essentially identical. The greatest difference in risk inclination between men and women is in physical risks, with men noticeably more comfortable with physical risks.
>
> The two types of risks for which women indicate a greater risk inclination than men are relationship risks and emotional risks. Of note is that women's general risk inclination increases for many women once they are beyond childbearing age.

As I talk about gender, I want you to keep in mind that our wonderfully complex brains and learning have affected everything we discuss here. And from a biological perspective, I also want to acknowledge that there are women who have more traditionally male behavior patterns, and *vice versa*. Simple observation bears out that fact.

As Jim's data highlight, young women are less likely to take physical risks, but I often get a sideways glance from young women in my class when I tell them why: I think the underlying reason is that it's their nature is to protect the egg.

An ovary typically produces and releases one egg per month; a female is born with every egg she will ever have. Given the premise that human beings are first and foremost designed for preservation of species, it is logical to assert that the egg is precious and the body gives us the instinct to protect it. We want to forget how important instinct is to us because it reminds us we are shaved apes. Males, on the other hand, produce sperm on a daily basis so there is no need to stockpile. One man can fertilize dozens of women easily. Men, unlike most women, are quite satisfied with taking risks if it gets them an immediate reward.

The next consideration in terms of behavior is that breeding for a female mammal is only the beginning of a relationship. She faces weeks, months, or even years of nurturing after that. Women are designed for nurturing. In contrast, breeding is a finite task for males: attract, breed, sleep. We can make elaborate plans to get to that end, but the end is just that. Without social constraints, males would not insert themselves in the nurturing the process. With social constraints—humans enjoy making life more complicated—males stay involved and help preserve culture.

If we assume, then, that breeding is a finite task for males and the beginning of a process for females, we can see there will be differences in the way we approach nearly everything. The long-term impact is that even when women of childbearing age are afraid, there is a part of them that instinctively protects the Holy Grail of the species: the egg. This behavior is all part of normal thinking and reactions, according to neuropsychiatrist and author Louann Brizenden: "The mommy-brain transformation gets under way at conception and can take over even the most career-oriented woman's circuits, changing the way she thinks, feels, and what she finds important." (*The Female Brain*, Random House, 2006, page 98.)

Step back several thousand years and look at the behavior patterns of our primitive ancestors. Males were the hunters out of necessity, not only because of our physique, but also because the females were either pregnant or tending the young. The male brain is also better suited to this type of finite-task thinking. We make wonderful long-range plans and stick to them. On the flip-side, we are not quite as good at making a flexible plan and constantly tweaking it to get a long-term result. Our male ancestors would have said, "There is this animal, who is always here at this time. Let us go kill it." The females would say, "Somewhere out there are some really good berries. I am not sure where they are, but they will be good with meat so let us go find them." This evolved into, "These berries are really good. Let's make sure that bush stays alive." Does that sound familiar? Is it any wonder that, through cooperation, the male and female brain came up with agriculture? The male brain conquered the plant by moving it; the female kept it alive. Granted, this is a simplistic look at male and female brains, but the concept does play out in our interaction.

Because we are shaved apes who do not want to be reminded of the hairy patches, my view isn't popular. But when equal opportunity advocates accuse me of chauvinism, I respond, "You are missing the point." To force a female to do things in male fashion is not equal opportunity, it is distorted idealism.

The impact of testosterone on our modern, highly developed brains should not be underestimated. Male brains do not develop the corpus callosum to the degree that women do, therefore, it does not communicate left to right with near the frequency or intensity of the female brain. The result is what women see as the one-trick-pony male mind. A woman will see many sides of the same equation as she looks for how to "nurture" the problem and create a solution. Another effect is that women are hyper-communicators and do so with many more words and much more nuance of body language.

Males tend to have clarity of focus on a single finite task, and as part of that focus, typically don't have high-speed, vibrant interaction between the left and right brains. When a female observes that plodding process and asks, "Why didn't you . . .?" and, "What if . . .?" one thought immediately enters the male mind: "Why can't you think in a logical progressive fashion: A,B,C?" This difference in thinking makes the male mind think the female mind is flighty, when in fact, she's processing creatively and logically in rapid succession. If men do not ask for directions, it is because we have a plan and we know that it is right from the beginning.

Just as the human skeleton dictates movement, the reproductive system plays its part in human behaviors and movements as well. This is never more visible than in children in the throes of puberty. A perfectly sane male child at 12 has lost his mind by 16. Suddenly, his brain has become more decidedly male and, as part of the process, is being outvoted two to one.

On November 1, 1986, when I was still with the Old Guard, our commander decided to bring a young female Marine who taught aerobics into our unit. The reason I remember the actual date is that most of us had been in the Georgetown section of Washington, D.C. for Halloween and a night of hard drinking. Aside from the fact she was very attractive and dressed in spandex, she had no value to the infantry unit. Testosterone filled the air as we scoffed at doing aerobics. Then the commander informed us that we could add old bowling pins to our routine, because he'd acquired them from the newly rehabbed alley. "Oh, great!" we muttered to each other. "Now we can look gay and dorky." This macho attitude lasted for about 10 minutes until this ultra-fit tiny blonde woman worked our asses into the ground. She told us in the beginning to use only one pin, but, of course, we were men. In the end, we hit total muscle failure.

I use this story to illustrate one thing: men and women move very differently. While we were making very large square movements in order to remain masculine, the instructor and the men who didn't care about being macho were making soft sweeping movements that used the energy of the swinging pins, instead of trying to control it.

The very nature of male movement is reflected in every part of our body language. When a man acts more like a woman, you will likely see superficial signs of female movement patterns, but the skeleton will anchor the movement in maleness.

With the physical and innately related mental gender differences in mind, let's take a look at some basics of human communication. A good starting point is the gestures I touched on in Chapter 3—adaptors, barriers, and illustrators.

Adaptors

One of the most powerful differences between men and women is in the use of adaptors. I use the word "powerful" intentionally. Men are tactile creatures who prefer to overdo everything. If one nail is good, two are better. Comedians have made careers around this. A dentist once told me that the leading cause of tooth loss among men is gum disease triggered by brushing too hard. My personal version of this is the inclination to take two vitamins instead of one. Fortunately, my brain usually overrides that idiocy.

As I noted before, adaptors are nothing more than the body finding a way to comfort itself in a foreign or stressful situation. Think of a coyote pacing in a cage. We find our own ways. A man waiting outside the delivery room will likely look very much like the coyote. What do you think is going on in the coyote's head? Is it any different from what is going through the expectant father's head? Maybe the actual content differs, but the process is the same— obsession with one thing. When the brain obsesses, the body takes over.

The male tendency toward the tactile means that men will transfer more physical energy than women in using adaptors. A man will rub his eyes hard in response to stress, whereas a woman will rub lightly beneath the eyes, almost in petting fashion. A common assumption is that women don't want to smear their makeup, but I have observed this type of touching in cultures where women don't wear eye makeup. It is as if the nurturing piece of femaleness even transfers to the self.

A woman who is uncomfortable will place the fingers of one hand in the palm of the other, thereby creating not only an adaptor as she lightly massages her fingertips, but also a barrier to close out the offenders. I watched Carol Burnett, now 73, do this very thing this morning on a talk show. She has been away from the limelight for a while and her discomfort showed. I noticed other signs of fight or flight during the interview, too.

A man in a similar situation will wring his hands; the effect is a masculine let's-get-down-to-business gesture while adapting and barriering. A man rubbing his legs is an inborn male approach to counteracting stress. As he rubs his thighs, the contact with his skin releases hormones to comfort him, while at the same time, the aggressive rubbing releases energy. This adaptor is not just for a baseball player on deck. You will also see it in the board room.

Women have a version of the batter-on-deck, too. I have sat in rooms with women who are suddenly "cold" as the meeting heats up. They cross their arms and pet themselves on the elbows and forearms. A learned behavior, it may have started in response to cold, but it has become a strategy for self-comforting and barriering. Because people actually do a variation of the move when they're cold, this tends not to draw attention to discomfort.

The energy transfer effected by adaptors varies from individual to individual and culture to culture. The variations are too numerous to list—this book would turn into a body-language encyclopedia. The one constant is that, typically, men are more tactile than women, which means men's adaptors are easier to identify than women's.

Barriers

A barrier shields the self from threats, whether real or perceived, and demonstrates the need for control. Closing your eyelids, changing your angle of approach, and other subtle moves belong in the mix of those you know well: using hands or arms, desks, counters, books, and computers to put something between your torso and another person. Your choices of objects to use are often subconscious. In proper male fashion, most personal non-object barriering is bigger for men and women. Remember how men think: a little is good, so more is better.

Most often, men move the barrier further away from the body. As a result, the barriers are more evident. These barriers will likely find themselves closer to the person's center of gravity as well. The exception to this is the fig leaf I described in Chapter 3.

Some barriers are meant to be impenetrable. Religious articles that represent faith cannot be safely tampered with; as such, they create the breastplate of God. Some of these barriers are meant for outward observation and others for internal reference only (for example, the Catholic scapula and Mormon temple garments). These barriers not only protect the wearer, they also tie the wearer to a commitment that takes priority over all else. You cannot overestimate the power of such an object. While outward representations are more acceptable on women in American culture, can you imagine arguing with a minister who is holding a copy of the Holy Bible as he critiques your immoral behavior? This specific class of men uses the object barrier more effectively than any other in American society. Most men have a tendency to rely on natural barriers.

If men use natural barriers more demonstratively, women use apparel and object barriers more openly. Take the woman who wears a 3-inch long cross. Is this primarily a symbol of religion or mostly a fashion statement? Put the same cross on a middle-aged man. What is the effect?

Illustrators

While men may brow-beat, women are more likely to make their points with the entire body. Because men have less of a tendency to engage the entire body and are less likely to gesture wildly, it is no surprise your third-grade teacher could get her point across without shouting. The illustrators used by men are typically uni-channel, such as hands, brow, or perhaps arms.

Even with the tremendous influence of hormones on the system, one cannot overemphasize the impact of nurture and all of the subprograms added to the human mind over the years a human is alive. Simply look at people who have experienced gender reassignment surgery to know that hormones cannot be the end of the story. Along with human behavior comes a concept of self.

Culture

Because men and women in the same culture confuse the body language of the other, imagine how easy this becomes across cultures.

Culture is like a ghost in the machine. Most cultural influences are so subtle we cannot recognize them. The long-term influence of being exposed to a culture alters our minds and behaviors forever.

Adaptors

Adaptors are the most natural, non-contrived body language that humans posses, primarily because adaptors are not intended to emphasize the verbal. They are for the individual's use only and most do not even realize they are using an adaptor.

Adaptors may be relatively consistent across cultures, but we can quickly make wrong assumptions if we look for something familiar. Just as false cognates in a foreign language (for instance, muwathif fucket—"Employees only " in Arabic), assumptions about the meaning of a gesture by someone from another culture will likely trap you in a misunderstanding. If there are so many forms of adaptors that we cannot list them here, imagine what can happen when viewed from outside a culture. Every culture will develop specific taboos and meanings whose origins have long since passed from memory. People in these cultures learn that the specific action is taboo by social norming.

Assume you develop an adaptor that is to rub all of your extended fingers and thumb on one hand together while turned upright. This looks somewhat similar to a gesture for money in the United States. Now, let's say your adaptor becomes one that places your other index finger in the cradle created by these extended fingertips. You do it frequently when you're under stress. Now put an Iraqi in the room with you and raise the stress level. His shock and anger would interrupt the meeting because he construes your gesture as a foul insult that questions his parentage.

If the impact of cultural taboos can limit your options on adaptors—truly involuntary gestures—imagine the impact on the more intentional gestures of barriering and illustrating. Male culture alone affects how American men illustrate their thoughts and barrier themselves. When was the last time you saw an American man purse his lips, hand on hips, flounce, tilt his head, and sigh to make the point of exasperation? That's Nathan Lane in *The Bird Cage*, not John Wayne. While any of pieces of body language alone may be acceptable, culture has taught most males that this is simply not acceptable male signaling. When we see this, it signals a different kind of male to the American eye. Male children whose primary caregiver is female may experiment with this signaling but quickly adapt out of it as their role models become male.

Barriers

Americans have a different sensibility about space and hygiene than most other cultures. Americans perceive an intrusion into personal space distressing, and that means any uninvited person needs to stand back at least arm's length. When viewing the body language of others, Americans may read more into a relationship than is really there simply by inference due to proximity. In the Arab world, however, men may even stand close enough for noses to touch. There is a famous news photo of an older Palestinian gentleman and an Israeli soldier within fractions of an inch of each other. The solider is shouting and giving the international signal for "get the hell out of here." At first glance, violence looks imminent until you see the older man has his hand touching the soldier—a sign they are beyond violence. The culture dictates that both men save face and it is exactly what is happening. The model of male interaction that I learned in Georgia would not include this message. I needed either an understanding of the Middle East or suspension of all I knew and a child's observation to understand the body language.

Taboos are so strong that we can project an image onto people based on our own interpretation of their body language. We even anthropomorphize animals to give their body language human meaning. How many times have you heard about a smiling dog? Our own definitions of what body language means transfers to other people and cultures as well.

The colors of culture

Even color is cultural and you need to consider it in reading body language. White means innocence and purity in our North American culture, but not many others. In Asia, white is the symbol of death. Black means authority in many cultures, such as American, but not all. Last year, I went to a science fiction convention in Atlanta to promote my previous book, *How to Spot a Liar*. An extremely tall man wore a strikingly accurate costume, complete with respirator, to establish his presence as Darth Vader. A friend told me that, after sharing the elevator with Darth, he found himself intimidated. "Why?" I asked. He pinned it on the impressive respirator and on past memories, bad memories, that the black leather and cloak symbolized. Would Darth Vader be intimidating in fuchsia? How about lime green?

Color has come to connote specific messages in cultures through the ages. In past eras, certain colors have projected wealth due to expense of production. There were even sumptuary laws to prohibit the use of selected colors, such as purple, as well as wearing decorated styles of clothing by anyone less than royalty.

The contrast with the practices of modern America is startling— if you were a Medieval lord, you would wander the streets of Detroit in shock over the colors used in clothing. We live in a world where an average American can buy clothing in any color he or she wants. We have evolved to a perception that anyone, literally, can dress like royalty. In terms of commerce, a practical effect of that shows up on Canal Street in New York City (or in sidewalk stations along Lexington Avenue, and so on) any day of the week. Peddlers offer copies of designer bags and shoes.

Americans are not unique in our desire to have what the more privileged have, with color being a key element in that distinctive look (for example, the little black dress.) We simply have easier access to the knowledge of what they wear and how to get it. We evolve culturally as a result of that awareness and consumer power. An important characteristic of our society is that we can form tribes on an ad hoc basis because we have the resources, creativity, and, for the most part, societal acceptance of clothing, accessories, cars, and even buildings with "new" colors: mint, sunburst, and dark chocolate. During the 1970s, if you were "in" as a suburban homeowner you crammed your new split-level with appliances in harvest gold and avocado. You were not "in" if they were still there 10 years later, though. Members of every subculture, such as the suburban homeowner, have their own symbols of belonging. Golfers have a look, or a range of colorful looks, that they can enjoy on the golf course and nowhere else. Horseback riders have their own look. Within the equestrian community there are even subcultures, as there are subcultures among suburban homeowners. No self-respecting dressage rider will be caught in cowboy boots, whatever the color. Even less likely is a real cowboy in cherry-red jeans. Each subculture will, through approval and sanction, create its own color and style code.

These sanctions and approvals can take many forms. Approvals come though the use of compliments, adoration, and sanctions, through means ranging from avoidance and unvoiced disapproval all the way to both formal and informal methods of humiliation.

The role of humiliation

Public humiliation as punishment, and mockery as a tool of intimidation are just two types of cultural practices that alter a person's body language with the specific intent of affecting his emotional state.

Whether intentionally inflicted or not, humiliation has an effect on the person's body language if endured often enough. Interestingly, it is impossible to predict what this effect will be. I've heard from numerous fellow redheads that they have felt persecuted; they talk to me with a wink as if there were some red-head cult that needed to rise up in solidarity. As I mention earlier, I even had one say to me, "We have to stick together! They do not like us because we have red hair." After wondering who "they" are, my response was a polite version of, "No, they do not like *you* because *you* are weird." These are people who have taken a bit of ribbing as kids and never outgrown it. Their humiliation is, at the point, self-inflicted.

A person who is humiliated continuously either allows the humiliation to become defining, as in the case of the persecuted redhead, or learns to adapt and is no longer humiliated when ridiculed. Take big-nosed Steve Martin in *Roxanne*. He learned to expect certain behaviors based on past experience. At the first indicator of what was coming, he identified a course of action he would take. He found ways to drain the venom from remarks that ridiculed his nose; the person poking fun would often become the brunt of the joke.

From the informal group all the way to highly formalized religious and national organizations, every culture engages in humiliation. Whether openly or subtly, groups rely on compliance to norms to help identify those who are undesirable. This creates a more homogenous society. We need ways to differentiate our monkeys from the other monkeys.

For the informal approach, watch kids in a school yard practice humiliation. The crueler kids—the bullies—perfect it as an art form until someone trumps them. This humiliation is part of the culture of the second grade (although a frightening number of middle-aged people act as though they're 8 years old). If you do not have the latest shoes, the right haircut, or proper social skills, you are chastised—childhood sumptuary law. There are a few reasons for this: first to create a more cohesive culture; second to establish a pecking order; and third, to learn and polish skills that will be used in adult life. Most adults are more subtle and polished, but every adult culture still has some second-grade rules floating around.

In a more formal act of humiliation, Saudis cut off the right hand of convicted thieves, not to stop them from stealing again, but to humiliate them. Their dining practice is to eat from a common plate, and only to take food with the right hand because Arabs use the left hand (often without benefit of toilet paper) to take care of business in the bathroom. Cutting off the right hand of a man cripples him socially.

What happens to the repeat offender, you might ask? Starvation? No, his fellow citizens will simply remove his left foot. With his left hand he can operate a crutch, but not attend too many social engagements. This may sound brutal, but Saudi Arabia has a much lower rate of theft than the United States.

One side effect of the interrogation process is the softening of a male prisoner's resistance before an interrogation as a result of the strip search. Even without an audience, the experience is agitating for most men regardless of nationality. Enduring this kind of display usually causes profound agitation. Contrast the reaction of an American Special Operations officer to stripping during interrogation exercises. As an American Army guy, I can tell you that having my clothes ripped off wouldn't make me give up any secrets. Culturally, it just isn't that big a deal and my movements during an exercise like that probably do not leak the slightest bit of stress. The U.S. military uses the locker-room mentality as the basis for hardening troops against the physical and emotional violations of their space and values.

Sanctions related to humiliating body language can take many forms. They come from avoidance and unvoiced disapproval all the way through blatant humiliation, both formal and informal.

Pop culture prejudice

In the 2006–2007 *Survivor* episodes filmed on the Cook Islands, the long-running reality TV show featured tribes segregated by race. At first, this jolted and offended lots of fans and foes of the series. As the idea got second consideration from many people, however, the pink elephant in the room became visible: humans do tend to go toward their own. If "your own" is visibly defined by features and color, then it's easy to find your brethren. In other words, in the thinking of the show's producers, if five African-Americans, five Asians, five Caucasians, and five Hispanics find themselves stranded on an island without the benefit of television cameras, there is a high likelihood that they will hang out with people of their own race *if* they have nothing more binding than race. Race can easily become secondary, however, to nationalism, or fraternal bonding such as common organizations or religious affiliation. It's an exercise predicated on the operation of tribal distinctions at their most basic level: "You don't look like me" or "You do look like me." One of the most succinct commentaries I heard about this was a tongue-in-cheek remark by one of the African-American pundits on the NPR show *News and Notes*. He said he was going to "root for the Black tribe."

Projection

In the beginning of this book I asked you to suspend the very thing that makes you human—your overdeveloped mind. Now we are at the crux of the matter. All of that programming given to you by your parents, school, religion, media, government, and personal relationships can cloud your vision to what you are seeing.

Projection means you see what you want to see. This is my operative definition, not a classical or clinical one.

I'll start with the elderly and disabled. We project weakness of all kinds onto a person who has any weakness of body. We refuse to believe that a frail-looking senior citizen can murder or that someone in a wheelchair could commit a terrorist act. And when we accuse someone like that of a crime, what are we upright, healthy folks likely to feel? Guilt. That's a big mistake—normal, but it's the same reason why a woman such as Aileen Wuornos could get away with murder. She was a woman. How dangerous could she be?

When we look at someone who is elderly or disabled, even someone who is young and sick, or "the weaker sex," some strong emotions may run beneath our responses and affect them. We see our humanity, our fragility, our vulnerability.

Part of it may be that that other person doesn't have the repertoire of body language that makes us feel comfortable. Subconsciously, we conclude that our own communication is curtailed by her physical limitations.

In writing this book, I wanted to do some people watching with Maryann on the street, in stores, at a coffee shop, and in bars. We were visiting with one of her friends whose home town bar scene could be characterized by the word "tame," but she thought one of them might have a little more action than others. Never having been there, we wondered how she arrived at that conclusion. Rumors. Hearsay. I had a feeling that a trip to one of the bars would help me demonstrate the effects of projection, especially how it interferes with a real understanding of body language.

Maryann's friend took one look at the waitress and thought she had her pegged. She read the tattoo, suggestive top, and sexy walk as signs of a certain kind of person. A very different person came over to meet us, however. The tattoo was of her children's names interlaced around her arm. Up close, the top looked more like a good choice for a hot summer day than part of a come-hither wardrobe. And I would not have called her walk sexy; that's a descriptor coming from someone who projected that an attractive woman with a tattoo and halter top would have a sexy walk. An accurate interpretation of the woman's body language would use words such as open, vulnerable, and attentive.

What is the ape in this photo doing?

(a) He's sucking his thumb to reduce stress.

(b) He's trying to tell you he has a toothache.

(c) He has his thumb in his mouth.

Eliminate any projection or conjecture from your evaluation and the only answer that's valid is (c).

Exercise

Do something similar to what Maryann and I did: Walk into an environment where you would not normally go. Depending on who you are, that could be a library, a bowling alley, a church, or a gym. Allow your projections to take hold as you observe people. Make a point of striking up a conversation with at least one of the people you have "pegged." Did you have any surprises and, if so, what did they tell you about yourself?

By nature, people filter everything we see and hear. This well-developed adult brain is constantly trying to put things in context, to create schemas that work in our world, to find patterns and connections. You must subdue that drive to be good at reading body language. You need to stop forcing things to make sense, and to focus solely on what people do and the similarities and differences between what they do.

Our lives are filled with rituals and routines that have made us successful or not. These strongly held beliefs and strategies color everything we see, hear, and do. Some of us have created elaborate tactics that prey on the rituals others have in place and I'll explore some very public examples of this in Part III. Trying to overlay all new information onto an old grid taints the information. Your filters will prevent you from seeing clearly.

Caricatures and stereotypes overemphasize at least one trait that people can identify easily about a person or group.

These super-typical mannerisms and cultural differences still exist, but outside of comedy clubs, it's no longer acceptable to use them to characterize a group. In an effort to honor diverse traditions and not hurt anyone's feelings—the long way of saying "be politically correct"—we've shoved most of these down society's linguistic garbage disposal. Ah! But out of sight does not mean out of mind. Though most of these have faded from public view, they still inhabit our conscious and subconscious. The result is a powerful filter that can blind the mind's eye.

Projection is the most dangerous blinder you can put on, and its real power derives from other things I talked about in this chapter—prejudices rooted in culture and gender. You have to ask yourself the question, "Which group of people am I biased against?" If you say none, you are delusional. You may be prejudiced against 5 ′ 3 ″ blondes who went to Catholic school and have perfect grammar. Not a bad group to most of us, but if you don't like them, you must identify your prejudice and look carefully at that group's body language if you want to communicate with them.

Other things can blind our vision as well, such as reading a book by an expert and taking everything at face value without adapting it to fit your own mind, personality, and the situation. This R.E.A.D. system means that you need to learn to look at a person and decide what something means when that particular person does it, and in a particular context. No book can do that. Relying on a laundry list of gestures and drawing conclusions, such as "hands on hips means…" are the worst kinds of projection.

What's likely to really trip you up, though? Think back to the "walking while thinking of a bad day" exercise. The emotional down shifted your posture and balance to low gear. Simply being in an emotional slump can profoundly skew your perception of another person's body language. No one likes you, so you're gonna go eat worms. You need to get past that down state, past your high state, past your own mood if you want to be really skilled at reading body language.

Making It Personal: A in R.E.A.D.

I have asked you to suspend your powerful brain and take in data similar to how a child would observe raw data without making judgments. I have also asked you to look for similarities and differences between people so you could begin to understand what is normal within a given culture or demographic. That's the "R." In this process of review, you taught *yourself* the second piece: evaluate, that is, look for the meaning of actions. You have also seen how your preconceived notions can filter what you are seeing, or even blind you.

Undoubtedly, you have begun to place people on bell curves to organize your perceptions. This is human nature, but it is difficult to research the chimps when you are one of them. You need a couple of other tools to help you understand exactly what this all means; namely, the individual's norm and context. These tools will help you to complete that final step of the interpretive process: "A," or analyze. Once you have analyzed what it all means, you can "D," decide how you will use that knowledge.

An individual's norm

When Data, the android on *Star Trek: The Next Generation*, has determined his chips have a glitch, he states that he is "not functioning within normal parameters." That's normal parameters *for him*. Even the quirkiest of personalities has a "normal" for him.

I am constantly asked how I can determine an individual's normal patterns if he is affected by illness or genetic aberration, for example. The answer is simple: I baseline.

I have a good friend who has Tourette's syndrome. When I first met him, it was a little disconcerting, but it soon became clear that as he becomes comfortable, his symptoms rarely surface. Within a few minutes, he won me over. I understand that he is okay with some not-so-typical, involuntary actions.

I learned to read his emotions and thoughts as well as I can read yours by taking two steps:

1. I turned off the filters related to health/illness and normal/abnormal that would have blinded me.

2. I paid attention to what is normal for him.

This is baselining. Baselining is a much simpler exercise with most people, although I can tell you that I pick up idiosyncrasies from many people who do not have a disorder. By now, you likely have seen a few for yourself, such as strange grooming behaviors, self-petting, or odd food rituals.

I started this book by defining communication and breaking it into vocal, verbal, and non-verbal. Let's use this model for analyzing what is normal for an individual.

Verbal: Servant of the will

Though verbal may be the servant of the will, occasionally the subconscious of a person will let you look into his mind through word use as well. Every person has a style of word usage that is normal for that individual. Because this book is a collaboration and my co-author ensures that my voice is maintained throughout, you probably have a pattern for my usual choice of words, and may even pick up a slight Southern accent, even though you cannot actually hear it. I am a straightforward speaker. I want to get the point across. I may understand many words that I choose not to use because I have settled on a style that fits my message. All people do this. Our choice of words is tempered by education, culture, self-image, and how we want to be perceived.

When someone's word pattern changes, you can usually track that change to a reason. If you are talking to someone who normally has a pattern of plain, simple English, for instance, and she shifts to an elaborate soliloquy about a product, what does that tell you? She read or heard some propaganda and committed a few phrases to memory. I usually want to ask, "Can you spell bioflavonoid?" or "What does germicide really mean?" When I first moved to Atlanta in 2000, I found a wonderful pub with hundreds of beers on tap. I had a favorite waitress at this bar, who reminded me of a young Jacqueline Bisset. Though unlike Ms. Bisset, she was not a bright light. When she decided to leave the bar for better pay, she mentioned the name of the restaurant. I said I had never heard of the place. She said, "Oh, it is a fine-dining establishment downtown." And those words came from whose head? One afternoon I was in the area and stopped by. Below the name of the restaurant were the words "a fine-dining establishment."

Similarly, the shift to simpler language can represent what is going on in a person's head. Perhaps she is dumbing down to play you—an old trick of some not-so-dumb blondes. Or is he trying to sound less intelligent to make you feel comfortable? You can also watch for length of sentence and pronoun choice to better understand a person's intentions, distractions, and so on. Pronoun shift from "I" to "we" can mean he wants to share the blame for something: for example, saying "We have to go now" early into a party that only he finds boring.

Vocal: Servant of the highest bidder

Vocal is the "servant of the highest bidder" because, under enough stress, the voice will sell out the will and tell you exactly what the mind contains. Volumes could be written about different tones and their meaning; everyone reading this book has heard these utterances. Remember your mother or some teacher wagging a finger at you saying, "It's not what you said, it's the way you said it!" I'm convinced that every day in every town, those words make it into the airwaves. If the human voice was the first musical instrument, it was also likely the first instrument of torture. Even a pre-human ancestor without a spoken verbal language probably got this point across with a shriek or grunt.

Stress causes a rise in vocal pitch. A stressed person will have clipped tones and a strained sound to the voice. Add a bit of heavy emotion—sorrow, anger, joy, uncertainty—and the vocal chords themselves respond similar to the strings of a musical instrument. Without any choice, the vocal has sold out to the highest bidder leaving the will to fend for itself with simple words.

Try this with your dog, cat, horse, or any other animal that responds to your voice: Tell her how much you love her in a gruff, angry tone of voice. How did she respond? Now tell her you are dumping her at the pound and use a happy baby-talk voice. How did she respond? People respond similarly. You sound loving, so you can't possibly want to beat me up.

I once worked with a SERE (Survival Evasion Resistance Escape) class for pilots. My partner for the interrogations was a tremendous Arabic linguist, so we interrogated one of the pilots in Arabic. As all good English speakers do, the pilot tried hard to communicate and struggled to find a word he recognized as we kindly and politely bantered with him about what a murderous bastard he must be. He tried again and again, and finally seized a false cognate from Arabic to English. We asked, "what is your name?" (In Arabic, "Esmuk eh?") Thinking that it sounded similar to "Smokey?" he made a universal symbol for smoking. We then moved to a much larger than normal condom he was carrying and asked him "Why?" in Arabic. Military people keep condoms on them to carry water, and he responded by trying to mime this. He started by holding both

hands about a foot apart top to bottom. We looked at him in aston-
ishment. Again in Arabic, we asked him if it was to be used on
children. He heard the word for children ("atfal") and seized on it,
thinking something innocent. He presumed we understood that he
would go to a waterfall and fill the rubber container. He then held
his hands up as if drinking from a large cylinder. Imagine the confusion and the result if this were real life instead of training. At no
point did he feel threatened because we had a friendly demeanor
and a light tone as we accused him of child rape. The false cognates confused him because he was looking for common ground—
projection, once again.

The best way to find out a person's baseline for normal vocal
utterances is to observe for a short period of time in a non-stressful
environment. In Prisoner of War terms, this means watching him
talk to other prisoners. In a prisoner's daily life, it may mean listening to mumbled conversations between cells—not for content, but
for tone. How does your boss sound when he is secretive, maybe
doing nothing more than telling his wife he loves her at the end of a
phone conversation? His tone changes as he fears how the simple
statement will be perceived by his subordinates. How does he
demonstrate he has lost his patience even when masking?

Non-verbal: Servant to the mind

Gesturing, typically under the control of the will, can occasionally break out of the cage. This is primarily because gesturing is a
learned trait, as is verbal, and, as such, is subject to rules about
common usage and taboos, just as the verbal is.

Symbols represent entire thoughts, so they serve as the clearest example of the correlation between verbal and non-verbal. They mean something specific in a particular culture and you can also express that specific idea in words. Quite understandably, then, this class of non-verbal is subjected to the same rules of control and outburst as the verbal.

Occasionally, a gesture may resemble something you know, so you assume it has the same meaning. Just as the pilot was trying to find meaning in the false cognates, you can easily confuse yourself.

All other non-verbal communication serves the mind, however, with little regard for the will. While the will of the young manager says, "Yes, sir!" to the boss, his mind places him above that kind of subservient response. The young man's hands give him away as he places them on his hips, similar to the young man on the cover of this book.

You want to look at the holistic view of an individual's body language while you notice the bits and pieces. If he projects an angry mood overall, but you see a playfulness about the eyes, what is the message?

If I were to see this in a very intelligent man, I would take it as a danger signal. The same signal coming from a middle-aged woman can mean something entirely different. Same picture, but different brushstrokes on the canvas. The only way you can be sure is by baselining the individual. For example, I may know that the woman's normal pattern relies on a ritualistic harshness when she's angry, but in this case, I see a playfulness to her eye and a softening of features. I may have a chance to win this one, I conclude; it is all in how I play it.

Now go back to the man with the same expression and compare and contrast the brushstrokes.

⇒ Does the person's body language holistically support the message he is trying to send?

⇒ Will his message differ when he's with the guys and with his mate?

⇒ Is his behavior similar to others of his kind? In other words, what is the norm not only for his culture, but also for males within his culture?

You have decided he is not exactly super-typical, but he does distinguish himself with certain gestures and postures. You have observed scalp to soles and mentally recorded data about clothing and other indicators of status. Next, you must discover what body language is unique to him.

Baselining mechanics

You need to ask questions that you know the answer to—a stage in your baselining activity whether you are hunting for verbal clues or behavioral clues. These should be simple questions that get his opinion about the best beer, or where to find a bicycle tire. Regardless of what the questions address, your aim is finding his norm, so you have to be non-confrontational at first. When he answers:

⇒ What is his normal way of looking around?

⇒ How does he stand/sit when relaxed?

⇒ At what level does he normally gesture—waist-high a little above the waist—and how would you describe his gestures when relaxed—open, energetic, and so on?

⇒ Where do his eyes access as he recalls data? (The test for memory versus construct is in Chapter 3.)

⇒ How does he respond when you ask about his opinion on a non-threatening topic, such as the best restaurant in town?

The responses give you insights, such as the following: After you have collected this baseline information, you ask him why Judy in sales flew to Vancouver last week instead of doing her usual site visit to San Diego. If he responds with facts, but his body language says "opinion," then red flags should go up.

Use the holistic approach to create a picture of what is normal for the particular person. This is not a month-long study of the monkey. This is a quick review of the person followed by an evaluation to note what stands out about this particular person.

We are all products of our environment, with culture playing an insidious role in the person we become. We get away with something, and it becomes a habit. We develop strategies for survival, and they work, so we repeat them.

Describe your habits and strategies. When you feel threatened, do you demonstrate your strength by becoming bigger, or do you shrink so that the threat will underestimate you until you can pounce?

The most successful among us have created many-layered approaches to communication and may broadcast strength and vulnerability at the same time to different audiences.

Baselining dos and don'ts

Do	*Do Not*
Ask questions that require a narrative response.	Ask yes-or-no questions.

A premise of baselining for eye movement is that your "source" must be forced to access certain portions of his brain, such as the visual and auditory centers. A yes-or-no question probably will not get the job done. For example, if your aim is to see whether his eyes move left or right to access memory, you would not ask, "Do you live on that street where lightning struck a tree last year?" You would say, "I think I know the neighborhood where you live. What are some of the landmarks around there?"

Do	*Do Not*
Sense and intuit.	Assume and project.

Your eyes and ears will collect a great deal of information, but what if those senses pick up "honesty," but you still feel something's wrong? Pathological liars, con men, and interrogators such as me have either natural or cultivated skills of deception. With us, you need to rely on intuition, too.

Women have an anatomical advantage because of having a larger corpus callosum than a man. This thick collection of nerve fibers that connects the left and right hemispheres of the brain gives women the practical benefit of signals crossing from the left (logical) to the right side (creative) of the brain, and vice versa, very quickly. In effect, women have a revolving door between the hemispheres that enables agile movement back and forth. Men have to open a locked door between them before they move to the other side. Intuition involves both feelings and facts, so you can see how the "female" brain supports it.

Assumptions and projections clog your ability to sense and intuit information about someone. Baselining is focused on one person at a time, and carrying certain assumptions as you go into an experience, or projecting your own behavior and style of communicating on someone, can give you false readings.

Do	*Do Not*
Take cultural and regional differences into consideration.	Let prejudiced notions and stereotypes affect baselining.

I'll refer you back to Chapter 2 to raise your awareness of cultural issues and differences. In short, pay attention to the many facets of the person you're baselining, but don't make snap judgments based on your biases.

Do	*Do Not*
Baseline deliberately, as needed.	Use the techniques habitually.

These are serious skills of an interrogator, not party tricks. You can save yourself time, aggravation, and heartache by using them in the early stages of dating, but if you start practicing on everyone, people will catch on and feel uncomfortable around you.

Context

What do you see in this photo? Is the woman blocking you out or simply standing proudly? Is that fist-to-hip gesture on the man an arrogant cocky smirk aimed at the photographer for a reason, or is it simply a pose? What about the kid sitting on the hood of the car? And why the distance? Take a minute without reading any further and decide what all of this means. As you read through the chapter, you will find the true story in the appropriate section.

No amount of reading can teach you to put things in context. If your husband came home covered in blood with his belt missing and told you he used his belt for a tourniquet to save a life—his head hanging down to the right and looking shaken—you would believe him. In contrast, if he came home freshly showered, in the same clothes he had on that morning, but no belt, and tells you the same story with his head hung down to the right and looking shaken, what do you assume?

Imagine the permutations. Now you get to engage your well-developed, adult brain by combining your newfound knowledge with years of human experience. You have reached the "A" in R.E.A.D., with an emphasis on the skill of putting behaviors in context.

Factors influencing context

Factors I want to highlight here are where the body language occurs, your subject's companions, and various aspects of timing.

Location

Where do you see the body language? Is it in a bar? At church? At work? In the airport? A car? Each will set expectations of how the person should behave. For instance, when driving in a car, do you pick your nose? I know some of you do because I have seen you. If a man's home is his castle, his car is his portable castle. People feel safe in this very personal space. Body language is natural; you can see exaggerated body language when a person talks on the phone when driving alone. Why? Most of us have brains that function well with only one or two tasks at hand—arguably, even the brains of the Millennial Generation that grew up multitasking with the aid of handfuls of gadgets. When you go past your task limit, something has to be compromised. It will likely be the high-end polished body language, as we forget someone may be looking.

The Airport

The airport has another pronounced effect because people are so disengaged from others. You walk from terminal to terminal, often without noticing others. The body language is artificial, in part because people are pack animals at the airport. You have the unnatural task of carrying or rolling an additional 50 pounds behind you and hurrying to make a schedule. Think back to the discussion of focus: If you are in the airport for the first time, or one of the first few times, you are still out of place and that shows in your body language. The seasoned traveler (at least the ones who don't thrive on anxiety) arrives with just the right amount of time to get to her destination; moving around the airport seems as comfortable as walking from one office to another. Regardless of the sensibility, the airport is not usually a social engagement.

Church, work, or other formal setting

Church may be the ultimate in formal settings with its rituals clearly defined. If it is the most formal for fear of retribution from God, at least God forgives; bosses rarely do. When I watched Sunday Mass from Notre Dame University as part of my research, I was struck by how many people followed the ritual, but looked thoroughly indifferent. Can you imagine sitting in front of your boss with this body language? If so, what about the CEO of your company? Is it natural for the alpha to make you uncomfortable? At work, the trappings of the alpha are omnipresent. Clandestine routines emerge so you can communicate things you do not want the alpha to see. How do you hide personal Internet use at work? Even when you behave naturally at work, you are displaying your normal work-self, not the person you are with a tribe of old friends or other microculture. Your body language will be more formal and less natural.

In an unknown place

When I first joined the Army, another 18-year old kid walked into the hotel we stayed in the night before our physicals. As I walked onto the elevator, he followed me with a halting, timid gait. He held his arms quietly by his side. "Everything okay?" I asked him. He answered, "I am from Buena Vista (pronounced "bewna vista" here) and I have never seen an elevator." Your uneasiness bleeds through when you are in totally unfamiliar surroundings and have no frame of reference. Even if you muster the nerve to act cavalier, your mind is still reaching for more data to create a familiar picture, and your body language will show it.

Companions

Friends, lovers, coworkers, relative strangers—your interaction with them affects how you present yourself, how much stress or raw emotion is present, to what extend your culture-specific gestures show up.

Opposite sex (which you may redefine as whatever sex attracts you)

Place one very attractive young woman in the presence of 10 heterosexual men around her age. What kind of body language will you get from her? Vulnerability and softening to look more appealing and feminine. From the men? Likely an exaggerated strut, hands on hips framing genitalia with overly blocky masculine moves. If this behavior yields rewards, what is the long-term impact for the person—either man or woman?

Super-typical people

When traveling with superiors, whether a boss or simply someone you perceive as super-typical, your body language will be constricted. Think of the expression "big fish in a small pond." The cliché refers to having the ability to be super-typical in a defined and confined environment. When you are the super-typical, your body language is uninhibited and expansive. When you perceive yourself as typical or sub-typical, you may limit how demonstrative you are with body language.

If being in the company of the super-typical causes you anxious moments, what happens when you are in the company of the sub-typical who appears to be super-typical? How can that happen? They know the routines of the culture better than you do.

Every year, Estes Park, Colorado, hosts the largest Scottish Highlands Festival in North America. On the fairgrounds, I saw hundreds of men in kilts and people of all ages in period costumes spanning a thousand years of Scottish history. I didn't think it was the least bit odd to see these people wandering around town in their outfits in the days just prior to the festival. The whole town was getting into the spirit and created a context for these people to broadcast their Scottish heritage.

In short, everyone wanted to belong, and many of the people who knew the traditions and had the right costumes—the people others tried to emulate—included those I'd probably label sub-typical in a different environment.

Antagonists

When a person is in a conflict of any type, the body language will show it. How fluid can your behavior be when your mind is rigidly set against the person you are standing next to? Not all antagonists arouse a sense of conflict, however. Some cause pain such as disappointment, frustration, or resentment.

That photo at the beginning of the chapter is my father, grandmother, and grandfather on one of my estranged grandfather's visits. He left weeks before my father was born and moved on to various other pastures, remarrying every few years. Envision the conflict and anger my grandmother felt when he finally showed up again—and this photo was taken. Abandoned by him in 1938, she was a devout Christian woman from the Deep South who suddenly had complete responsibility for two sons while pregnant with a third. My grandfather went out to get salt and came back when my father was a teenager. Now what do the folded arms mean to you? She had worked in the Georgia cotton fields to support her sons; my grandmother was physically and emotionally strong and proud. Why is he standing so cocky? Can we write him off as a callous philanderer, a selfish and self-indulgent nomad? This is a man who, at the age of 35, went ashore on D-Day with the 29th Infantry Division. To some extent, that earned him the right to look cocky. Why does the kid look quietly pleased? Well, he's happy that dad is home.

The body language of conflict would look much different from what we are seeing here. This photo captures resentment. She may stand near him, but he is definitely feeling the cold shoulder. These two people lived on the same street less than a block away for years before his death and never even waved to one another.

Time

This is not just a time-of-day or time-of-year issue, as in Christmas Day or a birthday. Time as a factor in analyzing context relates to the way a gesture fits into a whole sequence of actions. When did the action you are analyzing take place, that is, what gestures preceded it and followed it? How long did it take to complete the gesture?

If you've ever seen a silent movie, in which movements seem faster than normal, you've observed the influence of timing on the meaning of a gesture. An actress portraying grief will put her head down, bring it up to talk and cry, put it down again, and repeat the process. It looks funny instead of sad to us, because the speed makes it look as though the grieving widow is bobbing her head up and down in a "yes" gesture.

Consider the range of possibilities in this example: A young woman smiles at you, but breaks eye contact quickly. Is this enough information to make the decision about approaching her? Does the type of smile have greater significance than the duration of her glance? How important is where her eyes shifted after that?

Now consider the range of possibilities created by this kind of eye contact: A young man smiles at you and stares. It is a friendly smile, but without any brow movement, so he doesn't recognize you.

He continues the prolonged eye contact for what seems like an eternity, even though it's only 10 seconds. How important is the type of smile in this case? Is your normal reaction fear? Anger? Annoyance? Curiosity? What other factors of timing in his body movement affect your response? If the young man bore multiple tattoos, and was wearing a beat-up hunting jacket, how would you react if he quickly shoved his hand inside his jacket as he stared at you? Now take this same young man, tattoos and all. He gives you a lingering stare with a blank face. The jaw is slack; his eyes are focused somewhere beyond you; his gate is ambling and disconcerted; and his skin, pale. These are signs of shock, and his sense of timing will be way off—so far off that even if he does do some of the same actions as the person I described previously, your reaction would probably be curiosity or sympathy, rather than fear.

Personal strategy

Humans have an ingenious ability to find what works. Once we discover what works, we use it until it doesn't.

When you were a child, the first strategy you learned was to shake your head to stop something from happening. You used that until you discovered the word no, which you probably repeated until your parents wanted to throw you in the trash can. In short, it stopped working for you.

As "no" failed, you learned other strategies to stop things from happening. You never completely discarded the old ones, you simply put them away or incorporated them into your much more polished scheme.

As your age and your intelligence about how the world works matures, your strategy for dealing with the world evolves as well. Because each of us is a unique collection of genes and experiences, this strategy is unique as well.

The real art to reading body language and thus analyzing (the "A" in R.E.A.D.) what something means, is to learn to vivisect these strategies and see the rituals, adaptors, barriers, illustrators, and gesturing for what they really are: a language specific to the person who is using it.

Your experiences and knowledge will give you a unique ability to do this. You have the skill to see the minutia as a child would, a model for the holistic, and the understanding of context won from years of living. Now you need to use those tools to look at the communication strategy of your subject. How much of what he is saying with his body is intentional? How much involuntary? Are the two aligned? Which is the most reliable?

In the next chapter, I will focus your attention on communication strategies of people in the limelight to see what works for them. At least most of the time.

Applying the Skill

P A R T

I I I

Politicians, Pundits, and Stars: D in R.E.A.D.

Every time a person is rewarded for a behavior, the behavior becomes entrenched. The toddler shakes her head "no." It works. She does it again and again. Adults are those children covered in more layers of life. When something works, you keep it in your repertoire and build on it.

When you hit conflict or simply need to influence someone, you revert to a successful model. Some of these behaviors will be conscious and intentional, and others will be adaptors that have worked for so long they become second nature. Here are a few strategy models. Look around you and create your own list based on what you observe, so that it becomes a tool for you to use in the "D," or decide, of R.E.A.D.

Strategy Models

The intentional or unintentional behavior a person relies on for conflict and influence has a downside that gives you clues to what is really going on in his head: the model is not all encompassing. The supporting body language is often missing. You can detect irregularities. When the model does not work, the person may flounder in attempts to be convincing.

The Holy Warrior

This person creates an image that is beyond reproach by bonding to a Cause. Simply being associated with the Cause assuages his guilt in other areas. If you manage to attack his behavior, he will quickly become indignant—chin up, enunciating more clearly—so that you understand his point of view because, obviously, you must have missed it the first time. He stays on topic, which is the Cause, and off of topics or discussions that raise questions about whether or not he has the knowledge and skills to say what he's saying. This is commonly used by the moral hijackers among the super-typical, who understand little about the whole issue, but lift themselves to the role of saint for the Cause.

I'm Just a Girl

This is most often used by women in a male-dominated industry. Younger women might also use it successfully against someone who is matronly and self-consumed. The woman can play up the most feminine of her characteristics and emotional (weak) body language to look vulnerable and more feminine. This body language plays on the innate ability to make men more protective and less fierce. She plays up the "I'm just a girl" to get men to either cease attack or influence behavior in some way. Many women have perfected this in personal relationships as well by quietly allowing the men in their lives to believe they are in control.

The Flirt

He or she may rely on a variety of behaviors, and not necessarily sexual ones. In my dictionary, flirting means making emotional contact with someone, and filling the air with energy. It can be done between the same sex or opposite sexes. You know you've encountered a flirt when, regardless of how far you are from him physically, he seems close. There is no dead air between the two you. A skilled flirt can connect with dozens or even thousands of people at the same time, with each one certain that the connection is personal. Some politicians do it through speech and some musicians do it through song. A big reason why movie and TV viewers can feel attached to stars is the artificial closeness that the camera creates. The flirt takes your mind off of everything except the interchange. You suspend looking at body language and may not even notice content.

As an interrogator, flirting is a requisite skill. I believe anyone can learn enough to be an expert on any subject in two hours or less. All you need is an understanding of where the issue intersects the person—a skill inherent in flirting. If I can understand what about your profession keeps you up at night, you and I have an emotional connection. You will overlook hygiene, dress, and mannerisms in someone with whom you can identify. After all, when you have that connection, anything negative about that person reflects on you.

There Is Nothing to See Here

This can have several variations, the simplest of which is self-deprecation to the point that others underestimate the person. I use this most effectively when wearing boots, jeans, and a baseball cap. My slight Southern drawl can become quite pronounced. It is a skill every Southern boy has seen an old Southern lady do at least once in his life. This is play on a stereotype—remember that filter? Once someone writes me off as stupid I can then relax my guard and do whatever I need to do, assured that people rarely change their first impressions.

I'm Just a Kid

Similar to playing on femininity, a young person can play naïve and uninformed easily with a self-consumed person who is older. This is the simplest for young people to pull off because their body language is likely less polished and fits the profile.

The Blamer

He or she preys on the fact that no one likes to be accused. Human nature drives you to deny or defend, which focuses all energy internally looking for that fact or plea that will change others' minds. This ploy successfully blinds the eye of an opponent; it is one strategy that is difficult to fight. You need to pause and watch the accuser's body language to know whether it is a ploy or an actual attack the person thinks has merit.

The Magician

This has overlap with other strategies, which are basically variations with the same objective: If I can take your eyes off my body language for a moment, maybe you will miss the facts. Nevertheless, I separate out the Magician because there is an entire class of people who use movement of hands, feet, and objects to mask body language entirely. Examples are the guy who moves in very close and whispers to make you feel uncomfortable. The distraction makes you miss the rest of his body language. Or the woman who unfastens a few buttons so you can peek at her surgeon's handiwork. These outrageous moves will accomplish the goal of taking your mind off something else. A person may even use some other prop such as a Rolex watch. All use your tendency to keep your eye on the ball to effect the desired result.

The Car Salesman

He or she subscribes to the adage "If you can't dazzle them with brilliance, baffle them with bullshit." Everyone has met the guy who sounds as though he has swallowed the *Guinness Book of World Records*. When his strategy works, he carries off the same sleight-of-hand tricks as the Magician. It falls apart when you challenge his understanding of the facts he quotes. He takes you off a sensitive topic that would make him look bad by tossing out, "Every minute we do nothing in Vulgaria, three children die." He becomes adept at tying anything back to some obscure fact that is difficult to verify and only tangentially germane to the topic.

The reason a person akin to this survives is that most people are intimidated by his "knowledge" and the rest follow another well-known adage, "Never argue with an idiot; he will beat you down to his level and win with experience."

Again, the permutations are tremendous. The thing they all have in common is a ploy to distract your mind from the obvious things a toddler would see, and to bring you around to his way of thinking. Build your own list of ploys. Here's one to start with: The Ringmaster: "I am so busy that...."

I want you to put your new categories to work by examining strategies of the rich and famous, and noticing when they fail as well as when they succeed. Elections, news, and red-carpet events will now have a new dimension for you. Instead of wondering why you feel distrust or disgust about a politician, you have the eye to spot verbal and non-verbal warning signs. And are the stars you love to love and love to hate really deserving of all that emotion?

US Weekly asked me to analyze Jennifer Aniston's body language during the flurry of interviews that followed the intergalactic publicity over her breakup with Brad Pitt. In observing her gestures, I concluded that she was too honest to hide her true feelings completely, regardless of what she said; it was refreshing. Suddenly a star I knew nothing about (I'm one of the 19 people who never watched *Friends*) differentiated herself from the other celebrities I'd been asked to critique because the role she played in interviews was herself. She came across as someone who would make a good friend. For real.

As I take you through studies of public figures, I encourage you to watch some of the same video clips on your computer that I reference here. See if you come to the same conclusions I did and, if you don't, consider how projection, gender (yours and the other person's), ideology, and other elements may have influenced your thinking.

The Clintons

Love them or hate them, both Bill and Hillary have successful strategies for putting off prying eyes. With two very different personalities, each adapted to a microculture—their personal relationship—that images of the couple together merely hint at. Ironically, they have managed to accomplish this cover-up while creating images as recognizable as the Kennedys.

In looking through her book *Living History* (Simon & Schuster, 2003), I see a couple with contrasting body-language styles: Bill, the life of the party, with his arm around Hillary, the grounded one. His focus: broad; often leaning towards her while maintaining the attention of the camera. Her focus: narrow; the cameras. A task-oriented person, she has an agenda and she knows what it takes to complete the task. Does this say one cannot be funny and the other serious? Or that one needs more approval than the other? Obviously not when we consider the Clintons' track records.

Bill Clinton

The former president is not *a* flirt he is *The* Flirt. He defines extrovert. I know a few people who have met him and walked away enamored of him, regardless of political leaning. One man who met him on a golf course said, "It was like talking to someone you have known all your life, and like he was focused on only me while we spoke." He is never distracted openly and intently focuses on whomever he is speaking to. This has kept him alive. He fills the air and takes distance away, in part through solid eye contact, but in equal part through solid use of illustrators and regulators, as well as a persistent smile. He is smiling—whether his face is smiling or not—and there is a certain childlike enthusiasm in his voice even when denying infidelity. He has a natural charisma and the ability to make everyone feel as though he is connected to him or her. I read a bipartisan poll (for what it's worth) that answered the question "Who would you rather have a beer with: Bush or Clinton?" Guess who won. You never noticed his body language, even as he whipped the American psyche with his figurative riding crop as he declared, "I did not have sexual relations with that woman…." His charm takes us away from the body language that would tell the truest of stories. The strategy is a perfect fit.

Hillary Clinton

In analyzing Senator Hillary Clinton, I found riveting contrasts in body language between her and the person she criticized as "heartless," pundit Ann Coulter. It is as natural for Senator Clinton to use the word "heartless" to define an enemy soldier of the right as it is for Ann Coulter to use the word "Godless" in describing the elite of the left. Both are sensationalist ways of inciting the emotion of the typical.

By the way, I cringe in using "sensationalist" about Hillary Clinton's speaking style.

To describe Hillary Clinton's style as anything more than wooden or mechanical, you would need to see her "on cause." The first thing I notice about her speaking style is the tether to the text, whether her statement is a few sentences or a few pages. I do not think she is always reading, but rather barriering herself. Regardless, her habit of "reading" has invited criticism, including a recent jab from Former Defense Secretary Donald Rumsfeld. In a Senate probe in response to the secretary, Clinton once again read her brief comment from a prepared statement and he took shots at her because of it. She held her lips pursed, and had the tone of voice of a prim grammar-school teacher as she chided the secretary for his and President Bush's failures. Hillary at her best. How can you respond to her attacks? This is about you, *not her*. She represents the *truth*. This energy sent a clear picture of the Holy Warrior prepared to do battle for what is right (actually, "correct").

In watching speech after speech, I rarely saw her raise her center of gravity from behind the podium. She moved along precisely enunciating every word, as though she needed to be understood by one of those automated bill-paying systems. She gestures and uses her hands appropriately enough to get her point across. Facial features also reflect a congruency with her speech, and, occasionally, she even leaks a little emotion. When she is "on cause," though, she springs to life. She can take on the role of smug Holy Warrior in an instant. Her body armor becomes the issue she is supporting, whether it is the defeat of a voucher system because some parents will want to use it to put their kids in a Jihad-focused school, or removal of violent video games from children's hands.

Her stress surfaces in a move I typically see in heavy people. It's a shifting of weight from one foot to the other in an adaptor I call the elephant shuffle.

Despite her quirks, Hillary Clinton has created an image that many Americans seem to prefer. She can call someone from the right "heartless," because the hard right has a difficult time connecting with average people. But here's the irony in terms of her body language: while her message is one of warmth and caring, her demeanor shows neither.

Ann Coulter

When she's among friends, being interviewed by conservative acolytes, right-wing pundit Ann Coulter projects confidence, and her wit flows with very little hesitation in voice or body. Even there, however, when she isn't in the middle of a strafing run on Democrats, you'll see her run her hand through her hair and fidget a little with her fingers, which she usually keeps laced as a control mechanism.

Years of being "the girl" among a bunch of college Republicans and later inside the Washington, D.C., Beltway has given her a strategy that clearly uses her gender and physical attractiveness to her advantage. Lets face it: how many other ultra-conservatives do you see who have pitched battles in a little black dress? When she is among her admirers she tilts her head occasionally with a soft, amused smile, and she pushes her long, silky locks back over her feminine ears as a reminder that she is the pretty girl among the troglodytes of the hard right. She often laughs at her own punch lines. Between that and playing with her hair, she comes across as artificially girlish. This is response to a culture where she is a unique creature.

Part of the problem in trying to catch Ann Coulter's body language when she is not in control is that so many of her interviews occur with men who adore her. Smiling at her through her own self-amused ha-ha-ha. She's the golden-haired beauty of conservative men, the sex symbol of the hard right, and they generally don't ask her tough questions that might make her nervous. When they do, she does what she says she hates: ignores the question or changes the subject. She then punctuates her dismissal with a hand wave and a little more laughter. If this is her body language among friends, does she use it in the enemy camp as well when attacking or being attacked?

That's why no analysis of Ann Coulter's body language would be complete without looking at her appearance on *Hannity & Colmes*. Alan Colmes may not be the toughest player on television, but he does stand proudly as the liberal counterpart to Sean Hannity. On one show, she finds a quote that Colmes uses so offensive that she bursts out an accusation that he's lying.

Not surprisingly, he takes it as an insult and counters her. She talks over him while her flailing arms, raised voice, and random words show she is out of control. She quickly employs all of the "I'm just a girl" moves in her repertoire, none of which work. Alan is bolstered by a fellow liberal and goes after her. A sharp shift in body language signals her discomfort, and a stream of girly, dismissive gestures and nervous laughter follow. These are body language for "I'm trying to push you away. I'm trying to push your ideas out of the interview." She physically leans closer to the conservatives in the studio as if to say, "Help!" Even to the casual observer, her deliberate lean away from Colmes would project that Ann Coulter's whole being no longer wants to be anywhere near this ideological threat.

During her *Godless: The Church of Liberalism* (Crown Forum, 2006) promotion tour, a stop on the *Today* show also brought her into conflict with Matt Lauer (whose tiff with Tom Cruise receives attention later in this chapter). First, her "uniform" for this interview and many others seems to be a sleeveless black dress that is the same (or similar to) what she wears on the *Godless* cover. Facing Lauer, with two-thirds of her long legs showing and the tips of her blonde hair brushing her breasts, her presentation made the point that body language includes choices of dress and grooming. It was obvious that she was doing something analogous to what she accused the widows of 9/11 of doing. Their dead husbands are assets in making a political point, and they used them. Ann Coulter's assets are legs, hair, and wit, and she used them.

She inserted her points effectively in the interview until Matt Lauer made one unsettling comment. Coulter had insisted that the reason these widows served the liberal cause well was because they couldn't be challenged; that would come across as mean and inappropriate. "Well, apparently you are allowed to respond to them," he said simply. She suddenly became a supplicant, with hands in an almost begging posture. "Well, yeah, I did," she responded.

He kept at her, pushing until she finally burst out: "You're getting testy with me...awwww." Arousing the audience with that remark (and probably dividing the audience) marked the beginning of an attempt to boomerang back into control. Her body language invited her admirers to close ranks around her in a virtual sense. Even the best strategies do not work all of the time.

George W. Bush

Contrast Hillary Clinton's rarely off book style with President George W. Bush's often critiqued shoot-from-the-hip style. He swaggers when he walks, as any good cowboy would. He is often working without a net and says things that the media finds worth mocking. Whether you actually like him, or just listen for what he will say, his body language projects a genuineness, and generally remains on track.

His style also fails him. Uncertainty as to how a specific point will be received, or whether he may have flubbed a fact, causes an involuntary response that I call the goofy country-boy smile. His face—not his mouth—is asking, "Does that sound okay?" Time after time, I see him search his head for the right words—the prepared words—in response to questions. When he is on the hot seat, he starts to rummage though his mental files to access the words some expert on his staff gave him. The result is a somewhat halting, often piecemeal-sounding response. Most of the Bushisms come as a result of a "right church, wrong pew" kind of statement. He has researched and prepared a great response and it is filed neatly in his head; unfortunately, he put it in the wrong drawer. When he realizes his goof, he feels the pressure increase, and leaks the stress with comments such as "Too many OBGYNs aren't able to practice their love with women...." Because he has been in the public eye for a good portion of his life, he has adapted a self-deprecating sense of humor, and is often underestimated as a result of employing it successfully. It's a keen use of the There Is Nothing to See Here strategy. One does not have to be Einstein to pretend to be less than he is.

Mark Foley

As I write this, Mark Foley (R-Florida) has just resigned after his dirty little text messages surfaced in the news. In reviewing ABC News footage of him from an earlier interview, I noticed a body-language giveaway. When questioned about legislation he sponsored for exactly the kinds of crimes of which he is now accused, he said, "These people need counseling, they certainly don't need to be in... (pregnant stammer) interacting with young people." All the time his brow lifted to extremes. Was this a call for help?

Nixon and Kennedy vs. historical memory

What do you think of Richard Nixon?

Although it isn't possible for most Americans of the Baby Boomer generation, if they could watch Richard Nixon without bias, they would be charmed and surprised. They would subliminally recognize the synchronicity of his gestures and message, that is, his energy is focused in the same direction. The result is that they would perceive a genuineness, and in every video I have seen of Nixon—until the end when he morphed into a guarded, dark individual—that's what I see. The Nixon who ran against John F. Kennedy, served in the White House before Watergate, and opened doors with China projected congruency and truth, and was often rather unsophisticated about it. His strategy was What you See is What You Get.

Now turn the prejudice around so that it works in favor of the candidate. During that presidential campaign between JFK and Nixon, the Kennedy clan moved way out front into the limelight to help his cause. His brothers were out there, and even his mother took the spotlight, ostensibly dragging Jacqueline into it, as well. They were all Holy Warriors, except for Jacqueline.

One interview that featured Rose and Jacqueline Kennedy aimed to bring the American people "into the living room" during the campaign. How that ever worked to convince average Americans that JFK should sit in the White House is testimony to our naïveté as a nation. We are now so jaded by "candid" television interviews with candidates and their families that we expect them to be better actors, to decorate the set so that the majority of viewers will find it appealing, and to speak in the language of typical Americans. Almost no one else in America lived the way the Kennedys lived, but millions of people looked up to that family and carried a bias that their "royal" presence was a good thing for America—that it could lift us up. After all, if our most super-typical was so noble, what does it say about us?

The two women sat on a well-upholstered, uncomfortable looking sofa. Jackie delivered rehearsed answers to questions about the campaign—fluffy questions, not policy stuff—and Rose responded with stilted, puppet-like gestures. I wondered who's arm was in there making her head and hands do such odd things.

In another televised speech, Rose Kennedy was at a podium stumping for her son in a feather stole, and pearls that were more expensive that most people's houses.

Today, we would say, "What is this bull? Don't contrive things like this for us—we know better." We are a different culture with different cultural biases. Back then, however, we perceived the Kennedys as beautiful people, and felt that making them our "ruling class" made us all more sophisticated and beautiful. On the world stage, we as a nation were not beautiful people during and after World War II. The world saw power in the United States, but our dedication in war and strength on the battlefield did not change the perception that we were a bunch of scrappy rubes.

Celebrities vs. inquiring minds

After putting it off for months, I finally watched the notorious Tom Cruise interview that had been on the *Today* show. This is the one that moved him front and center as a spokesman for the Church of Scientology, and a critic of happy drugs.

Prior to the interview turning slightly confrontational, Cruise seemed to entreat Matt Lauer to understand his points about

Scientology and overuse of mood-altering medications. His hands took a position suggestive of prayer. It meant that he wanted to be understood. Before Cruise even specifically criticized Lauer for his comments on pharmaceuticals, I could see that his body started to assume the posture of someone who was going on the offensive—and I pointed it out to Maryann. "Watch this!" I remember saying. Just before Cruise launched into his attack on Lauer's ignorance with "You're here on the *Today* show..." his body moved into position. By the time he reprimanded Lauer for spouting off assertions without doing his homework, Cruise's body was lecturing Lauer every bit as much as his words. It was an example of perfect congruency. To me, that was a sign that his movements were genuine and unrehearsed. Score one for Cruise.

Mixed messages

In an episode of *Sex and the City*, a 25-year-old female admirer of sex columnist Carrie Bradshaw asks her if she can send her something she's written. Carrie vigorously shakes her head from side to side as she says yes. About a minute later, the same young woman asks her if she can "assist" her. Carrie vigorously shakes her head again as she says yes. Carrie is a New Yorker, part of a culture unto itself; a committed head shake means, "You must be kidding. Of course not." But Carrie is too polite to let those words come out of her mouth.

Politicians do this, or some variation of it, all the time. In other words, they don't achieve the ultimate in communication: synchronicity of speech and gestures.

In watching Senator Barbara Boxer (D-CA) address the Senate relative to the renewal of the Voting Rights Act, she showed a lot of incongruous body language. It looked as though she had determined that a static posture behind a podium wouldn't work for television, so she threw in a few arm gestures that had nothing to do with honest expression. That's not to say her words weren't genuine, but the artificial movements subtracted honesty points from her presentation. Similarly, her voice and words occasionally came across as incongruous. The most pronounced disconnect was when she said, "You don't have to thank me," in relation to the efforts to renew the legislation. Her pause at the end combined with a lilting pitch conveyed the exact opposite message: "I've done something important. You really should be thanking me."

Senator Boxer also reverted to steepling when she didn't know what to do with her hands. This is a posture with the fingers outstretched and touching; an upward point displays confidence and a downward point displays supplication or deference to another person. Which posture did Senator Boxer adopt? Supplication.

In all fairness, we shouldn't leave the discussion of Senator Boxer without noting that she pulled most elements together and projected real passion in speaking about her own proposed legislation, the Count Every Vote Act. Her illustrators were hitting her words in the right place, or, in lay terms, her gestures matched her words and emotions.

The endless campaign

"We should have done it," is what Senator John Kerry (D-MA) responded when Bill O'Reilly challenged him on July 20, 2006, about not coming on the show during the heat of the presidential election of 2004. Senator Kerry might as well have added, "You believe me, right?" because his raised brows and the lilt at the end of his sentence indicated request for approval.

When talking about a sore point that he needed to address—in response to a direct question about signing on with a colleague to censure President Bush—he tilted his head. Discussing a move similar to that would elicit a bit of emotion when done on the conservative Fox network.

Bill O'Reilly, a master of both asking questions and suggesting answers with his eyebrows, showed an important shortcoming in probing an "unfriendly" (that is, liberal) guest such as Kerry. He blockaded the possibility of reading body language—and really putting Kerry on the spot—by driving on with his prescribed agenda. In quizzing Kerry about the situation in Iraq, therefore, O'Reilly followed the pattern of questions he had in mind to ask. So where Senator Kerry asserted that certain things could be done more effectively, O'Reilly should have read Kerry's body language, which indicated some uncertainty. The simple question, "How?" could have proved very telling—but he didn't ask it. Instead, he plowed on and missed a prime opportunity to embarrass Senator Kerry, or at least shake him visibly.

Senator Kerry remained on firm ground, and then delivered a message: "I've never suggested pulling out too early," with arrogance and disgust expressed through raising his chin while he looked down his nose. To viewers, even many viewers who distrust him and despise his politics, he would have projected confidence and superiority.

"Fighting the war on terror more effectively, and that includes preventing Iran from having a nuclear weapon. Now how do you do that? Let me tell you." Kerry's measured pace in saying the first phrase stood in sharp contrast to the rapid, "Now how do you do that?"—almost as if it were a single word. And when he followed the question with the offer of an answer, he used a powerful illustrator: arm outstretched with palm upward. This is a classic gesture indicating, "I'm magnanimous. I'm going to give you something."

O'Reilly wouldn't let him give anything, though. He used a regulator—hands up like a stop sign—to put himself back on top. It allowed him to ask another question first, a tactic that would interrupt the flow of Kerry's presentation and undermine his momentum.

Ah ha! Kerry was too clever for that. He shut O'Reilly out again by driving on with his point and using his face: he narrowed his eyes and essentially "closed" his face. He was speaking, not inviting anyone else to speak. His subsequent tone of voice projected an image of educator more than politician, with face and body communicating to O'Reilly as if he were a kid back at St. Bridget's Catholic School.

It looked as though the senator might be back on the campaign trail.

Actors playing themselves

David Letterman's interview with Johnny Depp on July 28, 2006, revealed something interesting. It seemed apparent that Depp is, by nature, an introvert.

During the interview, he touched his face occasionally, usually by stroking his moustache, or flicking his nose. A couple of times, he also ran his fingers through his hair and tapped his crossed leg with his fingers—a leg that stayed crossed with the left ankle resting on his right thigh in exactly the same position throughout the interview. I see that as an attempt at control while his face and right hand leaked emotion. He had a litany of adaptors.

Depp seemed genuine—his fidgeting an expression of his true personality. So, I'd conclude he was himself on the show. He didn't bother to portray a character, as many other introverted actors do when they subject themselves to late-night talk-show banter. I'm sure you've seen some of those actors who try to make up for the fact that they are uncomfortable by taking on the role of entertaining guest; they come across as fake.

All of the famous people I have discussed have one thing in common: they evolved a strategy by trial and error. Each of them probably started very similar to you by a simple shake of the head and a later answer of no by your parents when you wanted something. Every time they met a new situation, they evolved their repertoires until the strategy was at its current state of polish. At some point we all stop polishing. The more public among us polish for longer than the more anonymous, all because of constant stimulus.

None of these survival strategies is right or wrong. What works for one person with his extroverted quick wit will not work for the systematic, thorough introvert. By now, you have enough information to analyze for yourself. For most of us, analysis of the famous is passive, meaning we will only watch body language and have little opportunity to influence the body language of the kind of people I profiled here. In the next chapter we will discuss the man in the street, so, we will start the conversation with some active use of body language or how to mange a situation using your body language to influence others.

The Man in the Street

Up to now, most examples I have given you have been passive. Or have they? Unless you observed strangers with absolutely no interaction in the review stage, you affected your subjects in ways you may or may not have realized. Simply because you share a microculture or culture with those people, your approval or disapproval impacts their behavior and body language. Though you may not think of it as such, conversation is a form of approval or disapproval. If you didn't hide behind plants similar to some distant anthropologist during your reviews—if you behaved normally and entered into some level of discourse with those you studied—then you affected them.

Gifted conversationalists such as Bill Clinton keep the flow of discussion going naturally by picking up tidbits that the other person leaks. In the world of interrogation, we call this information "source leads." We all leak these facts, opinions, and reactions; they help people bond to us in conversation. If you don't do that, then you're the one at parties who no one wants to talk to. Artful conversationalists use that information to direct and manipulate the chit-chat with questions, hints, sighs, and body language.

Exercise

Stand alone at a party, but make eye contact with someone you know. Give him 30 seconds and glance again. Does the person come over to talk to you?

As the conversation starts, stay focused on the person's topic, all the while nodding your head to affirm that it's riveting. When you have gotten most of his information, start to look at your watch somewhat secretively. What happens to the conversation? Quickly explain away why you looked at the watch without divulging the real reason.

Start the conversation back up. You have effectively used regulators to control the conversation. Nodding of the head makes the person think you are identifying with him and he feels validated. He will continue.

A second quick glance at your watch makes the person uncertain why, but certain that you have had enough.

While both nodding and checking your watch are regulators, the use is different. One helps you to *connect* and the other to *repel*.

With practice, you can send a message with body language that you have used only passively to this point. You can set out to make your own strategies. Unlike most of the world, you will be cognizant of every move you make as part of your strategy—without the need to have someone like me analyze it for you.

Most people connect through the use of positive body language, but you can just as easily use negative behaviors to force the person to feel as though he needs your validation. You must first review his body language, evaluate what is important and different, and analyze what it means before D (deciding how to use body language). Will you use positive body language to connect with him by making him feel like a kindred spirit? Or do you notice he is an approval seeker and determine that the negative approach through repelling motions will get him to struggle to win your approval, moving closer to you all the time?

Every interaction between humans changes the behaviors of both parties. When you are talking to someone, look for his strategies—for conflict and influence. Is it one of those discussed in Chapter 8, or something different? Mentally catalog these behaviors, because you will see that person use them again.

You are now moving into the sophisticated skill area of using your body language as a weapon. Be conscious of factors that will either support or degrade your efforts: filters, prejudice, lack of context, and wrong facts are a few. Just because you now know that crossing your arms does not necessarily mean you are shutting someone out, you can't presume your insight has rubbed off on other people. Most of the world does not get it; most people will make naïve assumptions and act accordingly. So use the more subtle techniques that I suggest here.

Mirroring

Mirroring to gain approval or to *connect* with someone is not the monkey-like mimicking of the person's behavior. In fact, if you are a man trying to mirror a woman, the mannerisms may differ quite a bit. Mirroring means getting the gist of the other person's mannerism. So if she places a hand on her hip, you may rub your thigh slightly to get your hand in a similar position. If she puts a finger to her lips, you may brace your chin with your hand. Both are thinking gestures.

Regulators

I often use regulators to start my source down the road to compliance. Something as simple as a finger across the lips to quiet the person is a powerful request. You then read the body language to determine if it is working. Conditioned response works to your advantage and compliance with your regulator early on is a reliable sign of it. Can you always use it to arouse a subliminal sense of "I should be quiet"? Definitely not. In some cases, use it only if you are in repel mode. Use it too obviously, and many people will see the gesture as the international symbol for "Shut the f*** up!" so honor the context. Be careful how you use it.

Adaptors

Some adaptors are best used when your subject understands a bit of body language. Tapping fingers and wringing hands send a clear message to even the least astute. I have used the tapping noise to draw a person's attention to down right, the field of vision associated with extreme emotion, to try to agitate him. My experience, while anecdotal, tells me this intentional move to evoke emotion often works. Other adaptors that can send a clear message are rubbing the eyes, cracking knuckles, and self-grooming as a ritual of boredom. The more subtle of adaptors, such as a slight finger rub, are wasted as a tool for telegraphing because so few people recognize them for what they are.

Barriers

Most people know a little about barriers. Remember the common—and probably your first—assumption about crossed arms? Typically, you use barriers as a tool for repelling. Most people instinctively feel shut out, and/or they feel inferior, when you use a strong barrier. Revisit the moment when you walked into your boss's office and faced a large desk. You sit exposed in a chair while the big guy builds his alpha status by sitting behind a hunk of mahogany. Real barriers are the trappings of authority.

You can use your extremities or objects that you carry to barrier and, conversely, to take down the barrier to make someone feel more welcome. Contrast this experience with the first: Walk into your boss's office when she invites you to step around the barrier and review her slide presentation. Suddenly, you are on the same side. As an interrogator, when I walk from behind the desk and close the space with a source, he never feels relaxed and thankful. The barrier provides a layer of protection for him. Context counts for so much in both understanding and manipulating body language—especially with barriers.

Illustrators

No one enjoys being brow-beaten during a conversation. Those Bill O'Reilly eyebrows or the wagging finger of Sister Mary Obedience cause a range of negative responses from "Go away" to "I'd like to have you hauled off to the landfill."

Careful use of illustrators can repel or attract. When Hillary Clinton is "on cause" and uses her hands in an uplifting manner, brows raised and passionately talking about entitlement, she brings the crowd toward her. Open, positive use of illustrators get the job done. When she is on target against Donald Rumsfeld, her illustrators become whipping motions with her hand, brow-beating with hands instead of her eyebrows. These are repelling instruments. The key becomes a question of, what are you trying to do? Connect or repel? Sometimes, you have to repel to get someone to bring himself closer to you.

Distance

Culture—from microculture through super-culture—dictates proximity in your interaction. In American culture, if you are intimately involved, standing far away can send a strong message of conflict. On the other hand, a casual acquaintance may be quite distressed if you move within 18 inches. Your intent again is either to repel or connect.

How do you choose to use distance? I know people who have told me that they have developed anti-hugger strategies to avert unwanted intrusion. The strategy may be as simple as a handshake or as complex as hand-talking that conveys, "Good to see you! We haven't seen each other in so long, we have almost become strangers." The combination of body language and words sends the message, "I like you, but feel uncomfortable with you that close." You can use your body language in this way to repel the person who is making the unwanted advance without causing hard feelings.

Timing

How quickly or slowly you respond is an indicator most people will recognize. A rushed answer can indicate urgency, especially when the answer is no. A slow answer can also be a negative when you use it intelligently. I can telegraph that I am unsure when asked for or about something by answering in a halting fashion. Women use this all the time, probably because many of you are trained to be agreeable, so giving an outright no is uncomfortable.

"Would you like to have dinner with me?" he asks.

Pause. "Well (pause), I actually have (pause) other plans," you respond. An astute man realizes you are saying, "No way in hell am I having dinner with you."

Managing stress

On more than one occasion in the interrogation room, I have used artificial stress or violation of cultural space norms to destroy a barrier between me and my source. The oddest part of this equation is that when I relieve the stress, the person feels thankful to me for relieving the stress I created in the first place.

Here's how it works in daily life. Maryann and I were walking from the grocery store one afternoon and talking, of course, about body language. I saw a slightly overweight lady a few years older than I am coming toward us. She was wearing a shirt that was too short for her body type, and a T-shirt underneath that exposed her midriff. By simply looking at the tail of the T-shirt and widening my eyes a little bit, I sent a message. Immediately, she began grooming, tugging the front of the shirt down. I turned away.

Let's take this situation to an end in which I really do want to manipulate her. I move in closer so she feels stressed. I say, map in hand, "You look like a local. Could you please help me with directions to the post office?" All the while, I'm looking her over. I then move in very close to her as I hold the map in a lateral posture with her. She now feels relieved because she thinks I was simply trying to decide whether or not she is a local. She has no idea why she quickly feels better.

This scenario shows how you can manage stress that you created in another person. Be very careful with this kind of interaction. Either you do it with finesse, or you may be headed for conflict.

Confrontational practices

In *Cannibals and Kings: The Origins of Cultures* (Random House, 1977), anthropologist Marvin Harris proffers four possible explanations for war. Even though he points out the reasons why each theory has holes in the anthropological big picture, the four views are salient in terms of categorizing confrontational body language, some of which is handed down generation after generation, and some of which just comes naturally. His ideas translate as well into the daily interactions of families and other microcultures. Unless we are talking about gang war or some such ritualistic conflict, we can assume that humans group into their armed camps in places such as office apartment buildings and even children's athletic events. The kind of warfare is simple conflict and it can range from catlike grunts and snarls to physical violence. Consider the reasons behind it and the body language of each.

War as solidarity

In this scenario, war results from a sense of group identity. The tribe that fights together stays together. In the modern vernacular, it's a street gang mentality. It can also be the third shift at the call center. Once you bond with other people who share your views and circumstances, you don't want to hurt your own. Aggression toward another group, even if those people share your circumstances, functions as a safety valve.

The chosen spokesperson may be super-typical, or perhaps a puppet moved to the forefront by the super-typical to confront. The purpose is to let you know that you have violated the tribe's territory. Maybe your crime is that you haven't refilled the toner in the copy machine when it was low. Regardless of cause, the body language is confrontational. If the issue is small, so is the body language, but if the issue is perceived as dire, the person's behavior may approach fight or flight. The gravity of the issue is dictated by the tribe's frame of reference. One common thread is the spokesperson's need for support from the group. If others are present, you may see darting eyes of uncertainty in the spokesperson as she looks for approval and reenforcement from the group—raised brows, wide open eyes as she looks at the rest of the tribe.

On October 24, 2005, Oprah Winfrey's interview with 9/11 widow Kathy Trant first aired. Her story of a "shopping addiction" to ease the pain of her loss had brought her infamously to the attention of the world. In asking her questions, Oprah's lilt at the end of her voice and raised eyebrows served as subconscious cues indicating, "Come with me into this train of thought, even though it might prove incriminating to you." It was Oprah's figurative way of holding Kathy Trant's hand and leading her into uncomfortable territory. Trant, whose spending spree included gifts of plastic surgery for friends—and obviously for herself—seemed Botoxed out of the ability to render normal facial responses. Even when she shed tears in response to Oprah's painful questions, nothing on her face moved.

The contrast seemed particularly sharp in view of Oprah's demonstrative eyebrows, eyes, and body. During a couple of exchanges, Oprah turned to the camera (the audience), widened her eyes and raised her brows, as if to say, "Do you believe her?" It was a request-for-approval look—and it's highly unlikely that Oprah made it in a calculating way. Nevertheless, it had the effect of drawing the audience intimately into the exchange. If Kathy Trant lied to Oprah, then she would be lying to every person in the audience.

In a meeting, I do what Oprah did, but deliberately. If someone puts forth an idea that I disagree with, I know I need to take specific actions to have the group adopt my plan as their consensus position. After the other presenter speaks, I might look around the table and say, in polite terms, "You're kidding me, right?" I'll raise my hands so that everyone is focused on me, with me. He sees that, and has to back down.

War as play

Is war just a competitive, team sport? All I have to do here is mention the word football, but I could add the pop-culture phenomenon called reality TV. The pleasure that some people get out of taking risks simply for the adrenaline rush of putting their lives, or at least their safety, in danger is the premise behind "war as play." The additional, cultural reinforcement to repeat the performance is the reward of accolades—hero worship. The same behavior plays out every day in offices and on children's soccer fields across the United States. Confrontation as play means we have less at stake even if it falls apart and we fail, we still get the rush and the conviction, "Maybe I will win next time." The children's soccer coach gets in the face of the referee, similar to incidents occurring at the Super Bowl. Most of the time, she knows she will not win. She confronts to confront. If this were her day job, would she get in the face of her boss with her paycheck at stake? Unlike a professional athlete being ejected from the field for insolence, her rude behavior will likely not affect her income.

Who has not participated in an argument for its own sake? Why are we willing to risk losing? Because in the process we gain as well. Whether we gain status, such as the small-town lawyer who successfully confronts a big-city litigator, or simply add another layer to our personality by honing our debate skills, the allure of "war as play" is there. The danger is that we may lack assurance that the other person takes it as play as well.

In this circumstance, body language is clear. At the outset, you feel you are right and justified. People do not typically enter conflict as a game when they feel terrified of losing—unless they have self-destructive tendencies. They enter chin-up, talking aggressively, energetic, and focused.

War as human nature

Do human beings have a killer instinct? Does each of us have the capacity for killer behavior—or at least confrontational behavior? I'll let the anthropologists slug it out over this one. What I know from experience is that human beings operate on a stimulus-response basis, and if the stimulus triggers an automatic aggressive reaction, even a pacifist (unless he's on par with Mahatma Ghandi) can't hold back. An interrogator will do this deliberately by synchronizing aggressive gestures and verbal attacks in an effort to bypass the source's cognitive functions, provoke his emotions, and keep going straight to his mammalian brain to get the basest response possible.

When humans enter into "war as human nature," only the most adept person can casually walk away from the outcome without long-term damage to the relationship. We use this one as a tool in interrogation because people will defend themselves when they feel threatened. Whether you think you have killer instinct or not, if I get in your face, scream, and call you a maggot, your animal self will rise up. When you go into a limbic mode (that is, emotional), you will simply respond instead of thinking. The results are clear from body language. Fight-or-flight body language surfaces: flaring nostrils, dilated pupils, elevated respiration, white sweaty skin, tensed muscles, and grinding jaw.

In this scenario, a great deal of the body language of confrontation will be involuntary, although not necessarily universal. You might use flailing arms or clenched fists without thinking about them, but these are gestures culture has ingrained in you as signals to arouse fear in the enemy.

War as politics

When one group attacks another to preserve or enhance its social, economic, or political interests, then war as politics comes into play. This makes particular sense if you believe that the unifying element of a culture is a shared view of quality of life, that is, what makes life good.

In some cases, what makes life good is status. Hillary Clinton and Donald Rumsfeld, as well as dozens of other people in the political arena, share a quality of life, and it is played out in countless interactions in the world every day. This is the politics of jockeying for position. People go at each other until one loses. Each enters the ring with an end score in mind, and has delineated what he is willing to sacrifice to get the concession. Often, the "winner" has the least invested in the argument; he can afford to take risks because he has less to lose in the long run. He can be magnanimous in letting the other have the ostensible victory. A powerful behind-the-scenes player is less likely to engage in this kind of open warfare. Men and women will also approach this differently.

Exercise

Watch a movie in which a mix of cultures and genders engage in confrontational behavior. A number of the James Bond movies qualify. Sort the body language by culture and gender. One way to tell if something is distinctly cultural is to envision someone with a different background using the same gesture. Would it either not have the desired effect or be funny instead of threatening? A good example is the pre-attack stance of a martial arts expert and the accompanying "Hi-ya!" You wouldn't run away if Chris Rock does it in his comic, mocking style.

Open your eyes to the conversations that go on around you—verbal and non-verbal. How much interaction occurs? How much of it is intentional? In the words of Carl Jung: "The meeting of two personalities is like the contact of two chemical substances: if there is any reaction, both are transformed."

Tread carefully on your acquaintances.

Using Body Language to Your Advantage in Business

Business is a subset of the rest of humankind. Think of it as a microculture or sub-tribe composed of people from multiple tribes who come together for a common purpose. Whether you are the receptionist or the CEO, you are part of a collective that shares a reason for being at work. In this process, you have to learn the social norms of others. Even if you are the super-typical, you still need to follow certain ground rules. You can change these through precedent, but even then, there are limits.

I start with this discussion because you need to be conscious of what the ground rules are for your tribe. Unacceptable behavior may get you voted off the island. Your first step is to assess the tribe.

Assess

Who are the super-typical at work? Are they all formally appointed leaders or, like an insurgent group, are there sleepers as well—stealth super-typical people whose influence outstrips their pay? I'll look at why that's important to know before examining how you can identify them.

Some people in the super-typical category get there by appointment or promotion, and then work all the way to the top. Achievement drives them. The alpha often has an I-love-me wall, or at least must be known as a high achiever in the organization. Everyone can sense this alpha's importance from body language, and the body language of others around him, so the situation is easy to see and easy to manage.

Other super-typical people in the organization may be less visible, but are just as important.

The influence peddler

The influence peddler sits behind the throne, perhaps without an official title, but with a network of associates who trust him and seek his advice. When he decides to heft his influence, he can make or break a project, timeline, or budget. He may only have the king's (or queen's) ear through complaints, but his power is vast. Unless the king removes him, he must consult with the influence peddler to reach the masses.

The advisor

Whether trusted by the king because he has saved his hide before, or simply because the king feels they are like-minded, he is the confidant of leadership. A difficult person to read because he may have no outward opinions, he is the most dangerous of the informal leaders: discrediting him means discrediting the king himself. Why was President Bush so fiercely protective of former Secretary of Defense Donald Rumsfeld? It called his judgment into question to allow the media to beat up Rumsfeld.

The instigator

The instigator holds no power, either official or otherwise. His only power is to stir up trouble. When displeased, he can cause things to go awry, and may not have the ability to undo the damage. In some cases, it is because he is a well-liked typical; in others, a quirky super-typical. In any event, his importance centers on his ability to derail your plans, so you need to read his body language for signs of irritation. Killing off the instigator does no good. The microculture will spawn another just like him. Your best opportunity is to co-opt him.

The coalition builder

This first-cousin of the instigator also cannot exist without strife. He finds a way to compromise all of the groups and convince them that they are happy with the outcome. The most successful coalition

builders manipulate with ease and either cause the strife themselves or allow it to fester until it reaches a point where all parties
must come together. He talks about everyone winning, which is
easy for him to say, because he is the only one truly getting what he
wants—resolution. The other parties lose in some way.

How do you uncover and deal with these hidden super-typical?
Keep these things in mind as I take you through the process:

⇒ The categories describe a select number of roles; you
   may have noticed others.

⇒ One person may fill multiple roles, or have solid
   identification with a single one.

⇒ The roles assumed by an individual may progress.
   For instance, an influence peddler/instigator may
   become the advisor simply because the alpha wants
   to keep him as close as possible for greater scrutiny.

The instigator

The instigator is the easiest to spot. While others suffer over
the latest mayhem, he shows smug pleasure—chin up, eyes comfortably open—as he surveys the outcome of his latest venture
with a glow of righteous indignation.

Some instigators are loud and obstinate. These will typically
only behave this way when they have someone in a compromising
situation, such as ill-prepared for a meeting or short on fulfilling the
terms of an agreement. The instigator will rarely launch a headlong
attack against someone who is prepared, which makes him more
similar to a hyena than a lion.

Most work behind the scenes and have the body language of secretiveness. They may instigate by sharing information or asking questions that get others to uncover the facts.

The best way to combat the instigator is to have him publicly endorse you, as in "keep your friends close, and enemies closer." Once the instigator endorses you—and this "declaration" may be solely in the form of body language that clearly realigns his relationship with you—he runs the risk of losing his credibility if he attacks you or backs away. You have something to hold over him with his co-conspirators. You have the key to causing public humiliation.

The advisor

You can also spot the advisor rather easily. This golden-haired child has gained the confidence of the king, so he can place his words directly into the king's ear. This has occurred either because the king fears his power or identifies with him. There are two types:

1. The *you're like me* advisor. You cannot win a head-to-head confrontation with an advisor in front of others without first pointing out that he is very different from the alpha. Disgracing him is a direct assault on the alpha, after which, the advisor can just step away and watch you fall. The only way to win the argument is one on one, or by first separating him from the alpha; that is, divide and conquer. This can come about by your playing instigator in open meetings: you ask questions that spotlight the differences to clarify the point to alpha. And then, once the alpha starts to ask the questions, you wait for the fireworks.

2. The *I'm keeping you close for scrutiny* advisor.
Already suspicious of this advisor, the alpha is constantly watching his back. You win in open confrontation with this advisor by waiting him out and asking
questions that will force the hand of the alpha. The
alpha cannot sit idly by as the advisor spouts rhetoric
counter to the alpha's thoughts.

The influence peddler

This person is the rock on which the company is built. Everyone owes him something, including you, whether or not you perceive it. He keeps a list and checks it twice. Easy to spot, he is the
social butterfly of the organization.

In my Army days, we called this a scrounger. In the old TV
show M*A*S*H, he is Rizzo the motor pool sergeant, who sells
stolen oil to get eggs for the chow hall, so Hawkeye can produce an
omelet to seduce the pretty nurse, so Rizzo can get penicillin
secretly to treat his venereal disease. This is energy intensive. Maintaining all of those relationships is similar to spinning plates on poles.
Because of that, the person is nimble in conversation, but less likely
to take the limelight. You will notice the influence peddler by preoccupation. The way to defeat him is to become the most important
cog in the wheel. Decide what the keystone is of his influence and
gently insert yourself into that position. The result is that he is no
longer important without your cooperation.

You only get close to this person with the body language of
helplessness—arms open, concerned brow, needy posture—as you

ask how you can resolve your problem. You will see their acts of magnanimity as they extend arms and enlighten you.

The coalition builder

You can spot the coalition builder because he is always helpful. Listen to him walk down the halls whistling his win-win tune. He moves adeptly between the opposing forces of the armed camps within the organization. Typically, he has the ability to see both sides of the coin and is not overly connected to either. He brokers arrangements, which are pure genius in compromise terms. The reason is simple: he loses nothing in the deal, so the win-win is his win. He sells the fact that he can create a truce and he does so by creating a solution in which both of the opposing parties lose some, but not all. King Solomon's ploy to determine the real mother of a baby was the ultimate coalition-builder move. (For those who are weak on Bible stories: Each of two women claimed a baby was hers. He said he would split the baby in half, which one woman agreed to, but the other asked simply that the baby be allowed to live.) Solomon, of course, resolved his dilemma more wisely than most by doing the right thing while exhibiting utter brilliance. The coalition builder is always the real winner in the situation. Opposing him is dangerous because the solution he represents is the one that makes the alpha happy.

The way to defeat the coalition builder is by having him identify with your cause as he describes his solution. At that point, if his solution has the potential to damage your cause, then his strategy becomes self-defeating. This is a difficult ploy because most coalition builders will have nothing vested in any outcome other than the alpha's desired one. Maryann saw this play out in a silly company fight over a logo. One faction wanted the logo in blue, and the other, red. The coalition builder knew that his boss preferred red, but someone from the blue faction casually caught the ear of the coalition builder: "Maybe red really is better. It's eye-catching. I mean, you see it on stop signs, police cars—it really makes you take notice." As soon as the coalition builder mentioned stop signs and police cars to the boss, he found lots of reasons to get people to rally 'round the blue.

So far, everything I have talked about in this chapter is similar to intrigue out of *The Prince* or *Dangerous Liaisons*, but it need not be. Can I use these tactics when in the presence of harsh negotiators? Yes. However, I much prefer the straight-forward approach I will detail for you here.

Shut up

In a room full of experts, I can appear to know more about a subject than you do if I sit long enough and listen. Here are the steps:

⇒   I watch your body language and illustrators. That tells me what really matters to each of you and what is ego.

⇒   I catch information from all of you.

⇒   At the end of two hours of wrangling, I have what I need to begin the distillation process. I can boil down the issues to the things all of you have said and agreed on, but not heard.

Your projection and filters blind you. I often use the Nothing to See Here strategy and dumb down your language a bit as I regurgitate your own thoughts. I suddenly appear to have the whole issue wrapped up. Imagine the control you could exercise with an immense amount of knowledge about a subject if you applied the same technique.

Never argue when you are wrong, unless for sport

If I play the devil's advocate for sport, I may take a losing side just to sharpen my skills. Otherwise, losing an argument sets a precedent.

If I win every argument, I seem to have secret powers.

How can you possibly win if you frequently argue when you are wrong? Only rarely would you want to engage in conflict for sport in the workplace. If you happen to be a professional negotiator it may boost your stock, but, for the rest of us, it is just dangerous. You may find yourself in the middle of an argument on the losing side without wanting to be there, though. At that point, read the body language of your opposing party and any other witnesses. How are they perceiving the contest? Is there a smirk of self-confidence in your opponent? Do the spectators support you or him? Do you notice a hands-on-hips gesture that projects his confidence that he has you where he wants you?

Noticing behavior similar to this, you need to choose your response based on the type of person he is: alpha, hidden super-typical, typical. You could respond by giving up and, depending on the circumstances, walking away. Or you could regain a measure of stature by waiting until you can make at least one point that shakes his confidence. While he is tabulating his answer, concede so as to leave doubt in his and others' minds.

Never argue and lose in public

Never voluntarily argue with someone in public. Early on in the Army, I learned to never counsel a subordinate in public. It is undignified for him and, if he happens to make you look stupid, potentially tragic for you. Also, never argue with a boss in public, because either you look stupid or he looks stupid and you suddenly look unemployed.

Unless no other option seems to exist, I keep arguments behind closed doors in a business setting. When forced to get confrontational in public, I will use dirty tricks involving body language, or interrogation ploys such as attacking the person's pride or ego to get him into a position of compromise. ("Someone as bright as you could not have meant that.") I may even resort to a little duck-season/rabbit-season logic shift to make my opponent look bad. For those of you who were deprived of Bugs Bunny, it simply means using the person's reasoning reworded to make him attack his own logic. When the argument is a matter of opinion, I just push him to rage and nothing looks as dim-witted as rage.

Catch flies with honey

The best use of these body-language tools in business is as an aid to understanding the real message someone is trying to get across. You can use them to create, rather than destroy, relationships, and they allow you to navigate more effectively among warring parties. My personality and training give me a tendency to see all points of view, which helps in finding the sore points for each person and achieving common ground to move everyone ahead as a team.

You are developing the skills to see what lies beneath—to understand what a person is feeling, but not saying. Use that to reach the person on a deeper level and understand the issue from her perspective.

Talk about the elephant in the room

When someone's body language screams, "I have a problem with you," but his mouth is saying, "Everything is fine," he secretly wants to get the problem into the open air. No one likes that feeling of pent-up frustration. The person will feel better about you for addressing the issue. People feel strangely obligated to those who relieve stress, even if they are the source of the stress.

Read the pauses and rushes

People leave pauses in awkward places and rush statements as a way of asking you to delve deeper. They may not be doing it on a conscious level, but these stops and starts are a request just the same. Listen for the non-verbal clues and look for the request-for-approval body language that says, "Are you going to let me get away with that?" or "You do believe me, don't you?"

Use the inclination of humans for social norming

Chapter 2 touched on the nature of humankind. The more often you conduct a meeting that is successful and everyone feels as though they are a valued participant, the more invested they become in your culture. As I said before, people do not go to war against people similar to themselves. You do not need some guru to have you fall backwards into each others' arms in a trust exercise to create a cohesive unit. The alpha sends the norms.

Look for patterns of behavior

Some patterns of behavior roll down from the top of the mountain and others sprout from the ground. Observe your corporate microculture so you know where the social norming starts.

Does your company have homesteaders (cubes that remind you of home) or crypt dwellers (stone cold, no photos or personal effects)? These external signs can be great indicators of the thoughts of people in your company, particularly whether or not they have a sense of trust and relationship with people. Does their body language reinforce your conclusion?

Be honest

A refreshing change, and a side effect, of your understanding body language is that you will be hypersensitive to your own behavior when you lie. You will notice every unplanned pause and wrong accessing cue. You will see yourself barriering when you do not want to be discovered. The stress can be unbearable.

Life is much easier after you know this. You will be predisposed to keep communication straightforward and honest. There is another one of those social norms I told you I would implant as a result of your reading this book. You are now stuck with this one.

By the way, the honesty I refer to here is common-sense honesty, not the radical honesty that compels you to tell your wife she looks like hell with her new haircut.

Your body language skills will not work office magic, or any other kind. Their advantage, which may seem to others like magic, is that you can know what the whole organism is saying. Every culture or microculture is its own, evolving organism. By watching the members of the hive you can see changes to the culture.

Using Body Language in Your Personal Life

Personal life encompasses a broad spectrum of relationships.

If you are married or in a committed relationship, you have a solid set of rules and expectations created by your two-person microculture. Best not to toy with them. If you are reading this because you think your partner violated one of your entitlements, I will tell you upfront: there are ways to use body language in a passive fashion to get at the truth and I will tell you what they are. However, if you are looking for the same kind of Machiavellian tools I covered in the business chapter so you can use them on your spouse, you will not find those here.

C
H
A
P
T
E
R

1
1

Sales

This is your body-language primer on dealing with salespeople or others who intrude into your arena. The best and pushiest salespeople, such as those timeshare folks, are usually reasonably good at instinctively doing what I am telling you in this book.

One of the best natural interrogators I have ever met, Mike Ritz, was a successful timeshare salesman before coming to the business. In fact, I learned and practiced some of the skills I detail here while at SERE and living near Myrtle Beach. I would get the free three-day weekend in exchange for listening to a 90-minute harangue. In the process, I would practice reading the salesman's body language passively and proactively to get the results I wanted. After doing this several times, I went to talk to a rep and admitted I was not going to buy. His response was predictable: you are committed to 90 minutes. I responded that it would be the most frustrating 90 minutes of his life. As I toyed with him by appearing interested to the point of closing and then jerking the rug from beneath his feet more than once, he asked me to leave and gave me lovely parting gifts. I had been wrong: it was the most frustrating *30* minutes of his young life.

When you do not want the intrusion of a fundraiser, salesperson, or door-to-door evangelist, use the combined body language of barriering that says, "I do not have time for you":

⇒ Crossed arms.

⇒ Looking at your watch.

⇛   Expressionless face.

⇛   Little to no eye contact.

The message this combination sends is a clear, "Go away." Of course, you could simply say, "Not interested," and close the door, but most Americans have a difficult time being that abrupt; we have a difficult time saying no. That is the second part of our complex personalities that we learn from our parents. After they teach us by positive reinforcement that shaking our heads will cause them to stop feeding us, then they teach us no is the word to stop doing something. As soon as we master no, however, they glare at us and say, "Don't say 'no' to me!" The message stays with us our entire lives.

Car dealer

A car dealer is a different breed of salesperson. Nearly no one goes to a car dealer casually, without intent. Knowing that, he uses the spider-to-the-fly invitation. He moves in for the kill when he sees the body language of excitement, or at least interest. I do not mean to imply that this skill reflects dishonesty. Some dealers genuinely want to serve your need for personal mobility. Others prey on those who know the least and take the role of advisor by becoming the expert. They tout safety features to new mothers and horsepower to young men. The trick with this behavior is to project what you want him to see and feign interest down several tracks to get him to use everything in his repertoire.

By doing this, you will know him inside out before you sit at the table to discuss money. Once you do sit, you will see familiar gears engage. He will try to maneuver, usually from behind a barrier. He will turn the contract around to you. Look at it for a few seconds. Use phrases such as, "From where I am sitting," or, "If you were sitting here, you would see what I mean" to suggest that he really would benefit in this deal if he understood your point of view. At the same time, use your body language to get him from behind the desk. Now he is in your court and you can negotiate more effectively.

Dealing with high pressure

Not all salespeople are high pressure, nor do all high-pressure tactics come from salesmen. Fundraisers, evangelists, people desperate for a date, and even friends, family members, and acquaintances can resort to high pressure to get what they want. This pressure usually involves some sort of bonding behavior that makes the person similar to you and makes it more difficult for you to say no to this fellow tribe member.

I have noticed this approach more and more in the prepared scripts used by telemarketers. One called me recently and began his conversation with, "Hi, Gregory, how are you today?" No one who actually knows me calls me Gregory. He then started to talk about the war in Iraq, and how many young men were returning from the war with body-shattering injuries. This move is bound to cause some reaction, whether you are for or against the war. My first thought was an anti-war fund-raiser. I was slightly amused that one would call me, but I held my tongue. In a great manipulative move, he asserted that if history is any indicator, many of these men will be on the streets in the coming years. Similar to many Vietnam veterans! He delivered a truly high pressure, emotional appeal to help homeless veterans. How was I supposed to deal with that one, being a veteran myself? He took me to common ground, incited my mind in preparation for a pro- or anti-war stance, and then shifted expectations to something few could argue with. The ploy was artful.

I turned the ploy back on him by telling him that I was an unemployed veteran. Okay, that's a half-truth, because I'm actually a self-employed combat veteran. The conversation ended shortly thereafter. I choose when and which charities I support and almost never make those choices on the basis of a phone call.

Although this pressure was on the phone, the same rule applies when dealing with high pressure in person. You have more signals and can read the person's intent and veracity more clearly, but the full-bodied press is harder to resist. If you do not know the person's baseline, ask questions and R.E.A.D. Those questions must be stress-free so you can ascertain what she does, how she speaks, where her eyes move while you simply chat. If you know the baseline, look for indicators. If the person is family or a real friend (more on that later), and in need of the requested amount or favor, sometimes personal sacrifice is in order. Do not just give in, though. You have the tools for uncovering need versus want.

When you decide you are not willing to give in or give up, use the momentum of the requestor against him. He has specific expectations that "x" will work. Let him think it is working, all the while nodding until you can see a flaw in the reasoning, and then point it out. The result is he has gone too far down one track to reverse course without loss of credibility. Most people will leave you alone at this point.

Friend or acquaintance?

This is the hardest distinction to make, primarily because of all the microcultures affecting us. Whether it is friend or acquaintance, we clearly share at least one microculture with the person, and each one adds layers of complexity to our personalities. Among my best friends, many are huggers, for example, and hugging signals that we are close. On the other hand, I have at least one very good friend for whom hugging would be bizarre. Differences in upbringing and experiences in life make us who we are. To confuse a reluctance to hug with a lack of affection would be tragic.

When an issue similar to this arises, ask yourself a couple of logical questions. Does he care about what is going on in your life? I do not mean the details of your life, but about your general well-being, what is making you lose sleep, and making you happy. You can read body language well enough now to tell genuine interest from perfunctory displays. On the other hand, a woman who is only interested in what keeps you awake at night may not be so interested in your overall well-being. R.E.A.D. Use everything you know, and overlay gender, culture, and context to decide for yourself.

The other question I often ask myself is, "How long can I go without seeing this person before something changes in the way I am treated the next time I see her?" If the answer is not long, then she is an acquaintance.

Dating

How do you approach someone you find attractive and determine whether or not she is available and interested? Some seem to have a natural gift for detecting this; others have the mating instincts of rocks. As a young soldier, I worked with another soldier who was one of the best-looking men I have ever known. He should have been able to attract any woman he met. And he would have if he'd kept his mouth shut. Unfortunately, when he opened his mouth, women walked away because crass and stupid don't appeal to most women. From my perspective, he was a good guy to hang out with. Why? He was chum. Not *a* chum, but the stuff you throw into the water to attract sharks. His good looks drew women in, and I could close the deal. More than once, I connected with a lovely young woman after she had turned away from his annoying open mouth. My success was in establishing some common ground.

To do this, R.E.A.D. to determine whether you are hitting or missing the mark in your conversation. Using the same skill set I told you about in business, simply watch for stressors in the person's speech and body language to find out where her passion is. If she hates something, and so do you, that is a better place to start the conversation than, "Come here often?" You may not, in fact, have anything in common, but you can start the conversation by at least appearing to care that she hates avocados. Mirror body language to make the person feel closer to you.

The next step you take is reading body language for signs of acceptance, if not attraction. You already know the basics for acceptance:

⇒ The opening of space to you.

⇒ Body language supporting verbal messages.

⇒ Timing and distance that signal "positive," that is, using body language to connect as opposed to repel you.

When you actually have a connection and there is sexual interest, your behavior should be in synch with your mood. Males have more of a tendency to speak quieter. Both men and women will have more blood flow to the mucosa, resulting in fuller lips and flushed cheeks. The pupils dilate to draw in more of a good thing. Both men and women may slow the rate of speech to be softer and more appealing. Unconscious mirroring becomes rampant. As a test to see where you are, consciously introduce an inconspicuous movement just to see if it is mirrored. If so, you have a green light.

Committed relationships

Many committed relationships start on faulty ground. There are no clearly defined expectations or entitlements. Most arguments, fights, and hard feelings result from one or both of the parties feeling these undefined entitlements have been violated. When this happens, because the committed relationship is likely the most emotional of our lives, the starting point of the interchange takes on an explosive quality. Remember: One of the thickest filters to see through is emotion. If you can back away from the emotional component and use the techniques I have taught you here, you can rise up to a level of success that will surprise you.

Given that every relationship is a microculture, you have developed rituals and subtleties of body language with your partner that are so obscure, no one else may notice. Your mate projects squarely what that raised eyebrow means when aimed at you. In some cases, perhaps the thought is very different from what it meant in the last fight, though—maybe the eyebrow is raised and there is a distracted half-smile. The review skills you've been honing will help you see that.

We all have trigger points that arise from years of baggage with a person who is very close to us. To take your new brush and paint over old wallpaper would be absurd and not productive. Use the tools first to understand. If you employ your skills in a ground-up way, you might actually notice something good rather than bad.

Turn 180 degrees. You want to use the tools to understand because you suspect something is amiss. Start with baselining.

Where do his eyes go when he discusses what he wants to do on vacation this year? If they go to the same place when you ask him where he was at 2 p.m. yesterday, you likely have cause for concern. Why? The first answer should be creative and the second one memory, with the eyes signaling access on difference sides of the brain.

Does his tone, cadence, posture, or barriering change when you get near a topic you are concerned about? If so, there is another cause for concern.

I go into much more detail about deciphering such behavior in *How to Spot a Liar*. One final thing to remember is that your eyes are jaundiced by emotion if you have gotten to this point. You will have a hard time being truly objective.

The best opportunity to get the truth is to use your own projected body language to express genuine concern and remind the person that you are part of the same tribe. Show that you matter, and that lying to you or mistreating you is painful. If you can come across as forgiving and willing to listen, and identify with your partner, you may get the person to confess his or her violation of your entitlement. If it is something big, then at least you have a factual basis for deciding on a course of action. Something small? Establish clearer expectations so that it never becomes something big.

I cannot say this often enough: Body language skills are not party tricks; they offer you a serious ability to improve communication and operate more effectively in all kinds of environments. Do not inflict your new tools on people around you. You will only make them nervous and possibly resentful.

Conclusion

P A R T

I V

Using R.E.A.D.

I keep yanking you back and forth between childlike observing and adult-brain thinking because you need to be agile in transitioning from one to the other in R.E.A.D. "R" requires wide-eyed, toddler curiosity, but you cannot accomplish "E, A, and D" without sophisticated mental processes and rich, human experience.

Right now, go back to the kid.

First, question everything I have said here. Always question experts. You are sitting in the best laboratory in the world—real life. No lab experiment paying people to participate in stress-causing exercises is going to produce the kind of stress a good butt-chewing from an employer will. No experiment about lying in which the consequence is a psychologist finding out can compare to hiding infidelity from a mate.

274   I Can Read You Like a Book

Second, keep your eyes open. Never take anything for granted. Simply because you see particular bodyd language on one person does not mean the same will represent the same thing on another. Gender, age, culture, and context play an important part in the body language from person to person.

Points to remember

⇒ Culture is pervasive. You cannot overestimate its impact on body language and on your objectivity in reading body language.

⇒ Long-term relationships are microcultures that create the most blinding of filters.

⇒ False cognates exist in body language, as well as spoken language.

⇒ Look for what is normal for the individual first. Baseline.

⇒ Build your own list of strategies and mood indicators. Those I listed are just the beginning. You have the tools to create your own tables and models for ready reference when you R.E.A.D.

⇒ Context is everything.

⇒ These skills require practice. Go practice.

⇒ Learn to turn the skills off when you do not need them.

⇒ *Review*: Look at the holistic, as well as the scalp-to-sole indicators. Take in every detail.

⇒ *Evaluate*: Know which one of the many pieces means more than the others.

⇒ *Analyze*: Use your powerful brain and overlay what you know on the grid of learned skills.

⇒ *Decide*: What will you do with the information? Will you call the person out and use your own body language as though it were a weapon, or simply make note of the behavior?

I have covered not only passive observation of body language, but also using body language proactively as a weapon. Be very careful with the latter application. Many young interrogators have gotten more than they bargained for by tapping into the hostile side of their human subjects. When people feel threatened, they lash out.

Remember how the process works. *Review* comes first for a reason. Simply by watching, you may find out you are dealing with someone who is genuine. You would not want to mess that up by engaging in body-language tricks that manipulate emotions. Conversely, you may discover that, based on his body language, he is an expert and far more dangerous than you want to tangle with.

The system is simple and not magic. It is based on observing and saying to yourself, "Now, why did he do that?"

Finally, you may be surprised by this advice: just ask. Having gone through this course, you are so much more attuned to what people are saying with their bodies than most other people, which you will gather tons of information in a straightforward Q&A. Ordinary conversation will give you most of the clues you need to read anyone like a book.

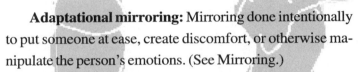

Adaptational mirroring: Mirroring done intentionally to put someone at ease, create discomfort, or otherwise manipulate the person's emotions. (See Mirroring.)

Adaptors: Gestures to release stress, and to adjust the body as a way to increase the comfort level.

Barriers: Postures and gestures we use when we are uncomfortable.

Illustrators: Gestures used to punctuate a statement.

Microculture: A subset of culture that may be as small as two people (for example, a married couple) or a large group, such as Texans.

Mirroring: A natural response to another person; gestures that reflect an attempt to assimilate.

Regulators: Gestures used to control another person's speech.

G
L
O
S
S
A
R
Y

Rituals: Habitual gestures that include such things as formalized bits of ceremony, microcultural norms, and idiosyncrasies.

Sub-typical: A person or group of people who fall on the left side of the bell curve in mapping a culture, tribe, or microculture.

Super-typical: A person or group of people who fall on the right side of the bell curve in mapping a culture, tribe, or microculture.

Symbols: Learned gestures that capture particular sentiments.

I
N
D
E
X

Abdel-Rahman, Sheikh Omar, 27
active observation, 115
adaptors, 68, 120, 170-172, 235
    culture and, 174-175
    gender differences and, 170-171
American culture, 43-45, 48-49
    homogeneity of, 50
anger as mood or emotion, 131
Aniston, Jennifer, 98, 214
anti-hugger strategies, 237
ape culture, 42
argue and lose in public, never,
    256-259
argue when you are wrong,
    never, 255-256
arms, the, 99-100
barriers, 68, 121-123, 172-173,
    235-236
    culture and, 174-176
    examples of, 121
baselining, 32-33, 188
    and context, 198-199
    and intuition, 196-197

do's and don'ts, 196-198
    mechanics, 194-195
    your partner, 269-270
baselining,
    the non-verbal and, 192-194
    the verbal and, 189-190
    the vocal and, 190-192
behavior, patterns of, 258
behavior patterns of our
    primitive ancestors, 167-168
behavior patterns, Texans and, 51-52
bell curve, culture, 38-39
bell curve to organize perceptions, 187
Bird Cage, The, 160
birth defects and the sub-typical
    role, 107
blink rate, 86-87
blocking, 145
body adornments, 108-114
body language and ritual, 17-18
body language as a weapon,
    233-234

body language, culture and understanding, 38

body language, holistic, 129-130
  direction and, 129
  energy and, 129
  foucs and, 129

body-language tools in business, 256-257

body language, understanding, 31-32

body movements, scanning, 33-34

Boxer, Barbara, 226

breeding for women and men, 166

brow and eyes in orchestration, 77-78

brow control, absolute, 78-80

Burnett, Carol, 87, 96

Bush, Barbara, 142

Bush, George W., 95, 221-222

business as microculture, 247

car dealer, understanding body language of the, 263-264

celebrities and social change, 48

Celtic warrior culture, 37, 42

Clinton, Bill, 215-216, 231
  and batoning, 118

Clinton, Hillary, 215, 216-218, 244

color, culture and, 176-178

communication,
  animal, 29-30
  definition of, 28-29
  human, 27-31
  non-verbal, 27, 28
  super-physical, 67-68
  verbal, 27, 28
  vocal, 27, 28

confrontation as play, 241-242

confrontational practices, 239-245
  war as human nature, 242-243
  war as play, 241-242
  war as politics, 243-244
  war as solidarity, 239-241

confusion as mood or emotion, 131

context in reading body language, 34-35

context, baselining and, 198-199

context, factors influencing, 199-205
  companions as factor
  influencing context, 201-204
    antagonists, 203-204
    opposite sex, 201-202
    super-typical people, 202-203

Coulter, Ann, 218-221

Cruise on *Today* show, Tom, 224-225

cultural norms and rituals, 124-125

culture, 19
  and adaptors, 174-175
  and barriers, 175-176
  and body language, 173-176
  and color, 176-178
  bell curve, 38-39
  of family, 59

culture,
  American, 43-45
  binding elements of, 37
  Celtic warrior, 37
  shock of a new, 59-62
  U.S. military, 144

culture shock, response to, 61-62
D'Onofrio, Vincent, 20-21
Data, 80, 188
dating, 267-268
Depp interview, Johnny, 228-229
devil's advocate, playing, 255
disability, impact of, 106-108
distance, 237
distraction as mood or emotion, 131
ears, the, 87-88
embarrassment as mood or emotion, 141-142
energy level, 148-149
excitement as mood or emotion, 135-136
experts, shut up in a room full of, 254-255
extremities, the, 102-105
eye
    droop, 85
    makeup, 84-85
    movement, 82-84
    twitch, 85
eyebrow, arching of an, 76-77
eyebrow flash, the, 73-74
eyebrows in "request for approval," 74-76
eyebrows, the, 72-80
eyelids, the, 84-86
eyes, the, 81-87
facial movements, 33-34
fear as mood or emotion, 137-139
feet, the, 104-105

fig-leaf posture, 102
    as barrier, 121
filter, gender as a , 164-170
filters, 163-164
flexibility as rounded movements, 149-151
focus and gait, 154
Foley, Mark, 222
forehead, the, 68-72
    wrinkled, 71-72
friend or acquaintance, deter mining if someone is a, 266-267
gait, 151
    focus and, 154
    lilt of, 154
    speed of, 152-153
    stride of, 153-154
Gates, Bill, as super-typical, 40
gender as a filter, 164-170
gestures
    and cultural context, 125-126
    and group evolution, 126
Gibson, Mel, 131
Godless: The Church of Liberalism, 220
gravity, movement and center of, 155-159
Great Depression, the, 45-46
hairstyles, 109-110
hands, 102-104
    grooming of the, 102-103
    secret signal with the, 103-104
handshake, American, 146
Hannity & Colmes, 219

Harris, Marvin, 239
hats, 110
Hayes, Sean, 52
head and neck, the, 97-98
head tilts, 97
high-pressure people, dealing with, 264-266
hips, the, 100-101
Hitler, Adolf, 35
Hohl, Dean, 60-61
honest, be, 258-259
humiliation and body language, 178-181
humiliation and kids, 179
illustrators, 67, 173, 236
and regulators, 117-119
illustrators, examples of, 118
interest as mood or emotion, 136-137
interrogation process, side effect of the, 180
intuition, baselining and, 196-197
jaw, the, 96-97
Johnson, Lyndon, 92-93
joy as mood or emotion, 133-134
Karr, John Mark, 80
Kennedy, Jacqueline, 110
Kennedy, John F., 92
and historical memory, 223-224
as the alpha, 46
Kerry, John, 226-228
Landis, Floyd, 97
legs, the, 101

Letterman interview with Johnny Depp, David, 228-229
lilt of gait, 154
limbs, the, 98-101
Lincoln as super-typical, Abraham, 45
lips, 92-93
licking of the, 92
location as factor influencing context, 199-201
airport, 200
church, work, or formal setting, 200-201
unknown place, 201
Lohan, Lindsey, 72
Martin, Steve, 179
McCormick, Jim, 165
media and the super-typical, 47-48
melting-pot concept, 44-45
microcultural rituals, 125
microcultures, 38
mirroring, 123-124, 234
intentional, 124
mood, 128-142
Morris, Desmond, 68, 79-80
Mother Teresa, 107-108
mouth, 89-96
covering the, 90-91
slightly open, 89
unconscious quiver of the, 91-92
movement and center of gravity, 155-159

movement, 151-159
    energy and, 160
    male, 169-170
    overall, 159-160
    patterns, 151
Mr. Spock, 76
muscle memory and movement, 157
neck, rubbing of the, 98
Newman, Cathy, 111
Nixon and historical memory,
    Richard, 222-223
non-verbal communication, 27, 28
    and baselining, the, 192-194
norm, determining an
    individual's, 188-189
nose, the, 88-89
O'Reilly, Bill, 226-228, 236
    and regulators, 119
Old Guard, the, 169
    posture, 143
openness and barriering, 147
openness, 144-151
"pain muscle," the, 71-72
passive observation, 115
pauses, awkward, 257
percentages and reading body
    language, 22-23
Peters, Bernadette, 96-97
points to remember, 274-275
posture, 143-144
    gender differences in, 149-150
prejudice, pop culture, 181
projection, 182-186
pupils, the, 82

Queen Elizabeth, 141-142
R.E.A.D., described, 18
reading body language, getting
    good at, 66-67
regulators, 67-68, 234
    examples of, 119
regulators in conversation, 232-233
relationships, committed, 268-270
reproductive system and human
    behaviors, 169
risks, physical, 166
rites of passage, 53-55
rituals, 124-126
Roberts, Julia, 96
role models, modern, 50
Roosevelt, Franklin Delano, 107
    as the alpha, 46
Rumsfeld, Donald, 217, 236, 244
salespeople, body-language
    primer on dealing with, 262-263
salute, military, 146
scalp-to-toe elements, 130
scarification, 54
secretiveness as mood or
    emotion, 139-140
SERE (Survival Evasion
    Resistance Escape)
    school, 11, 262
Sex and the City, 108, 225
shoes and body language, 111-113
shoulders, the, 98
smile
    of discomfort, 96
    of recognition, 95

smile, 93-96
  a real, 81
  balanced, 93
  camera, 95
  genuine, 93
  meaning of animal, 94-95
  seductive, 95
social norming,
  Civil War as, 44
  effect of, 54-55
  inclination for, 257-258
social norming practices,
  formal, 56-57
source leads, 231-232
Spacey, Kevin, 78-79, 80
speed of gait, 152-153
Stockholm syndrome, 123
strategy models, 210-215
  Blamer, the, 212
  Car Salesman, 213-215
  Flirt, the, 211
  Holy Warrior, 210
  I'm Just a Girl, 210-211
  I'm Just a Kid, 212
  Magician, the, 213
  There Is Nothing to See
    Here, 212
strategy, personal, 205-206
stress, managing, 238-239
stride of gait, 153-154
sub-groups within a culture, 51-52
sub-typical, the, 39-40
super-physical communication,
  67-68
super-typical, the, 39-40
  media and, 47-48

super-typical through the ages, 43, 44
symbols and gestures, 116-117
symbols, system of, 30-31
tattoos, 109
  cultural, 174-175
temples, the, 81
testosterone and the male brain, 168
time as factor influencing
  context, 204-205
timing as indicator, 237-238
Travolta, Johns, 22, 34
typical, the, 39-40
U.S. military culture, 144
ugly American, the, 49
utterances, 105-106
verbal communication, 27, 28
  and baselining, the, 189-190
vocal communication, 27, 28
  and baselining, the, 190-192
Vreeland, Diana, 112
Wayne and movement, John, 157
Will & Grace, 52, 100
Williams, Robin, 160
Winfrey, Oprah, 95
  interview of Kathy Trant,
    240-241
work, assess the super-typical
  at, 248
work, the super-typical at, 248-256
  advisor, the, 249, 251-252
  coalition builder, the, 249-250,
    253-254
  influence peddler, the, 248,
    252-253
  instigator, the, 249, 250-251

Gregory Hartley's expertise as an interrogator first earned him honors with the U.S. Army. More recently, it has drawn organizations such as the CIA and national TV to seek his insights about "how to" as well as "why."

Hartley has an illustrious military record, including earning the prestigious Knowlton Award, which recognizes individuals who have contributed significantly to the promotion of Army Intelligence. He graduated from the U.S. Army Interrogation School, the Anti-Terrorism Instructor Qualification Course, the Principle Protection Instructor Qualification Course, several Behavioral Symptom Analysis Seminars, and SERE (Survival, Evasion, Resistance, Escape) school. His skills as an expert interrogator earned praise while he served as an SERE Instructor,

285

Operational Interrogation Support to the 5th Special Forces Group during operation Desert Storm, Interrogation Trainer, and as a creator and director of several joint-force, multi-national interrogation exercises from 1994 to 2000. Among his military awards are the Meritorious Service Medal (which he received twice), Army Commendation Medal (of which he is a five-time recipient), Army Achievement Medal (which he received four times), National Defense Service Medal, Southwest Asia Service Medal, and Kuwait Liberation Medal. He also attended law school at Rutgers University.

Hartley has provided expert interrogation analysis for major network and cable television, particularly Fox News, as well as National Public Radio and prime print media such as The *Washington Post* and *Philadelphia Inquirer*. Important foreign media such as *Der Spiegel* have also relied on his commentary.

Maryann Karinch is the author of seven books, including the successful business book *Rangers Lead the Way: The Army Rangers' Guide to Leading Your Organization Through Chaos* (Adams Media, 2003). Others published works are *Dr. David Sherer's Hospital Survival Guide* (with co-author David Sherer, MD; Claren Books, 2003); *Diets Designed for Athletes* (Human Kinetics, 2001); *Empowering Underachievers: How to Guide Failing Kids (8–18) to Personal Excellence* (co-author Dr. Peter Spevak; New Horizon Press, 2000);

Lessons from the Edge: Extreme Athletes Show You How to Take on High Risk and Succeed (Simon & Schuster, 2000); *Boot Camp: The Sergeant's Fitness and Nutrition Program* (with co-author Patrick "The Sarge" Avon; Simon & Schuster, 1999); and *Telemedicine: What the Future Holds When You're Ill* (New Horizon Press, 1994).

Earlier in her career, she managed a professional theater and raised funds for arts and education programs in Washington, D.C. She holds bachelor's and master's degrees in speech and drama from The Catholic University of America in Washington, D.C.